I AM ME

by the students of Pleasant Valley School

PYP

Publish Your Purpose

Publish Your Purpose
141 Weston Street, #155
Hartford, CT, 06141

The opinions expressed by the Author are not necessarily those held by Publish Your Purpose.

Ordering Information: Quantity sales and special discounts are available on quantity purchases by corporations, associations, and others. For details, contact the publisher at hello@publishyourpurpose.com.

Edited by: Gina Sartirana
Cover design and interior layout design by: Nelly Murariu

Printed in the United States of America.
ISBN: 978-1-955985-70-3 (paperback)
978-1-955985-71-0 (hardcover)
978-1-955985-72-7 (Ebook)

Library of Congress: 2022911052

First Edition: November 2022

The information contained within this book is strictly for informational purposes. The material may include information, products, or services by third parties. As such, the Author and Publisher do not assume responsibility or liability for any third-party material or opinions. The publisher is not responsible for websites (or their content) that are not owned by the publisher. Readers are advised to do their own due diligence when it comes to making decisions.

Publish Your Purpose is a hybrid publisher of non-fiction books. Our authors are thought leaders, experts in their fields, and visionaries paving the way to social change—from food security to anti-racism. We give underrepresented voices power and a stage to share their stories, speak their truth, and impact their communities. Do you have a book idea you would like us to consider publishing? Please visit PublishYourPurpose.com for more information..

CONTENTS

DEDICATION

This book is dedicated to every child and their unique story, family history, and cultural heritage. If you have ever questioned whether or not you belong, the answer is yes. Each and every one of you belongs and is valued. Don't let go of the things that make you unique, for those are the things that bring us together.

We also dedicate this book to the adults in the community who promote and encourage inclusivity and equity to better support all of our children.

LETTER FROM THE SUPERINTENDENT

Dear Pleasant Valley Student Authors,

I am so proud of you and the amazing stories you have told in this very special collection of student voices! I enjoyed learning about you as an individual, as a member of your family, and as a member of the Pleasant Valley community. The students, families, and staff of South Windsor Schools represent a rich tapestry of cultures, experiences, and perspectives. As authors, your writings have now enriched this tapestry. Thank you for all you do as students to ensure that Pleasant Valley is a place where all students feel heard, seen, included, and have a true sense of belonging.

Dr. Carter
Superintendent of Schools

ABOUT THE I AM ME PROJECT

Pleasant Valley School is one of four amazing elementary schools in South Windsor, Connecticut. We are a community that celebrates diversity and inclusion, and this book was written to share the perspectives of students in one of our schools. The stories from our families and students share how unique each of us is while at the same time honoring the diverse tapestry of the community. Each story is told through the eyes of one individual in hopes that they will help us to understand one another, improve our practice and acceptance, and find beauty in the fabric of our community.

Recording our stories in this book allows us to capture each person's uniqueness and helps to promote conversations about our personal histories in order to better prepare for our futures. We honor the differences in each child and recognize that each child in this book will make a positive change in the world.

ACKNOWLEDGMENTS

Thank you to **everyone** at Pleasant Valley Elementary School and everyone in the **community** who has supported the staff and students during the writing of this project.

To our parents and students: thank you for sharing your experiences with us so that we may learn from each other. We hope you found value in the storytelling part of this project and that it has opened up a dialogue in your homes to share rich family history and discuss the hopes and dreams of your children.

To the amazing Pleasant Valley staff: we are fortunate to have staff who honor and seek equity and inclusion for the children in our care. Pleasant Valley is a special place because of each one of you.

To the building administrators, Principal Tiffany Caouette and Associate Principal Dr. Alicia Farris: thank you for the love and support you offer to the students, families, and staff at Pleasant Valley. You have made a tremendous impact in your time at the school, and each child benefits from your leadership.

To the Board of Education and Superintendent of Schools, Dr. Kate Carter: thank you for believing in and funding a wonderful school system that makes decisions based on the needs of students. Your support and dedication are felt in every classroom.

Pleasant Valley has always been a special place. Those who live or work in the community know it, and now we hope the rest of the world will know it too!

ABOUT PLEASANT VALLEY ELEMENTARY SCHOOL

South Windsor is one of the fastest growing districts in the state of Connecticut and one of the most diverse. Pleasant Valley Elementary School is one of four Kindergarten through fifth-grade elementary schools in town. The school has over 650 students, and more than twenty languages are spoken by our families in their homes.

We strive to ensure that **every student not only has the knowledge to succeed, but also is engaged, socially conscious, resilient, and empowered,** as outlined in the district's Portrait of a Graduate, a document that outlines the skills we want every graduate of South Windsor High School to acquire during their time in our care. Family and community partnerships, inclusion, and empathy are the cornerstones of our success. The South Windsor Public Schools' motto "Dream, Achieve, Inspire" captures our work in three simple words, which have the ability to change lives.

OUR STORIES

A PEEK INTO AADIT'S WORLD!

Hi! I am **Aadit Dhar Tarafder**. My nickname is Mizou. I was born on June 29, 2014, in Manchester, Connecticut, USA.

I like to play video games on my Nintendo, play soccer, and play with my sister and friends. I like to read comics and WHO WOULD WIN books. My favorite is the Tintin collection. I also like to watch the Pokémon Series on Netflix. My favorite foods are bacon, fish, and lobster.

My family loves to travel, and I've visited six countries: India, Canada, Spain, Greece, England, and Scotland. In the USA, I have traveled to many places, but my favorite is Washington, D.C. because I can see the important monuments and buildings that I have read about in History of America books.

My family is a Bengali family from India. Bengali people are from Bangladesh and the West Bengal State of India. Both my grandmoms live in Kolkata, India. My aunt (Mom's sister) lives in Virginia. My other aunt (Dad's sister) lives in New Delhi, India. Our main festival is Durga Puja which happens in October. Durga is the name of the God we worship.

Mimas is my little sister; her real name is Adwitiyaa. I gave her the name 'Mimas' which is the smallest moon of Saturn. She is fifteen months old now. She likes exploring and running, and she loves to play tag with me.

One thing I want to share with all of you is that my mom got very sick and was turning blind when Mimas was in her tummy. She had brain surgery and Mimas was born two months before she was supposed to. I was scared at the time, but I am happy that they are doing well now.

My goal is to be a good soccer player and play for India so they win the Soccer World Cup for the first time.

Me with my family last fall. I love this picture, because it is taken outdoors in our backyard.

I AM AADYA

Aadya Fnu

On the first day of August 2012, I stepped into this world. I was the new addition to my family, which made the first-time parents and grandparents so happy that they named me Aadya. The meaning of Aadya is first power, first to inhabit, or first to be at the beginning of the universe. I shared my birthday that day with my grandmother and the doctor who helped me to step into this world.

I was born in India, in the city of Nawabs where you get the world's famous Kebabs. I belong to a family that believes in hard work, compassion, and perseverance. My family's motto is, "Never give up." My favorite holiday is Diwali, excluding the firecrackers!

I enjoy eating sweets and visiting friends.

My favorite subject is math and robotics. I love solving multi-step word problems and programming. Apart from studies, I love music and sports. I am learning how to play the violin at school, and piano at home. The thing that surprises everyone is that I learned the piano myself! I play tennis, both table and lawn! I am a Pokemon fan. My Pokemon cards collection is currently 300, and I have inspired my dad to play Pokemon Go.

Now I'm coming to my creative part. I make Anime slideshows with my classroom friends. I have started to learn Manga.

I want to travel to different places, and the top destinations on my wish list are Dubai and Japan.

Now I'm coming to an interesting question: What do I want to be? Three years back, I wanted to be a doctor. Then I wanted to be an artist.

I don't know what jobs there will be when I grow up, but I know my passions are math, robotics, and drawing.

I am grateful to my teachers for teaching me and my parents for providing me the necessary resources so that I can achieve my dreams.

Well, this concludes my story. I hope you had fun reading it. Signing off. Bye!!!

I drew a Pokemon trainer, Mallow, with two Pokemon, Steenee and Bounsweet.

WHERE I'M FROM

My name is **Aarav Khedkar**. I was born on December 10th. I am six years old and in first grade! My school is the best!

I was born in Texas in 2015. A little while after I was born, I moved to Illinois. I don't remember it at all, but my sister says that we lived in Illinois for three years. My parents took a lot of pictures and videos of me when I was little.

Next, I moved to Connecticut with my mom, my dad, and my big sister. I only remember a teeny, tiny bit. I went to India and got stuck there because of the virus. I went to actual school in India for a few months before COVID came. I started having online classes when the lockdown started. They were very boring. During the lockdown, I started drawing. I practiced for months! Now, I can draw 2D and 3D cars. Sometimes I draw race cars. I also like to draw antique cars.

I have lots of small toy cars and monster trucks. When it is warm outside, I play with them in the dirt and mud and pretend it is a construction site. In India, we had a big garden with lots of plants. I used to water the plants with a hose and make a swimming pool for my cars.

Now, I'm back in Connecticut after being to all these places.

I feel like the world is my home!

My name is Aarav Khedkar. I've spent my whole life moving from one place to another! This is a drawing of me and my family and the things I like to do.

I AM ME

My name is **Aarav Surti**. I was born on December 23, 2012. I came home from the hospital on Christmas Day, and it also snowed that day. I live with my mom, my dad, and my brother. I like my name because it means "being calm and peaceful." My brother's name is Manav, and his name means "a good human being." Everyone in my family has a helping nature. I have two cousins, and they are my favorite, because we always text each other and just talk. They live in Canada, so we don't see each other a lot in person. One of my cousins is kind of like my twin; her name is Mansi. We have so much in common. We try to meet at least once a year.

My favorite sport is soccer. I think that I am very good at it. I also play it at my school. I have tried many other sports, but I liked soccer the best. Whenever we lose a game, my coach says that it is just a game and to try better next time.

My family celebrates a festival called Diwali. I really enjoy this festival because every year we do a Rangoli competition with our cousins. Rangoli is a colorful powder art drawn on the floor or the entrances of houses. Rangoli represents happiness, positivity, and liveliness and is also intended to welcome the goddess of wealth and good luck.

My grandparents select the best Rangoli, and my family has been winning for two years. I really enjoy being with my family. My family and I have had so many fun memories that we enjoyed together. **I love my family!**

Aarav Surti

My family Rangoli

Aarya Chauhan

I AM ME: AARYA

I am **Aarya Chauhan**. I am very proud to say that I am of Indian origin, was born in Kingston, Canada, and moved to the USA in 2018. I live in South Windsor, Connecticut, with my parents (my mom, Chaitali, and my dad, Vedang) and my sister Isha. My parents are from India, and we are a Hindu family. I love to celebrate Holi (the festival of colors), Diwali (the festival of lights), and Christmas. I really miss my grandparents and aunts and uncles and cousins because I can only see them when I go to India. I created a few memories with my grandparents when they visited us. The picture I like best is the one where I am pushing my grandmother in the swing.

My Mom told me that India fought for freedom against the British without weapons! The leader of Independence was Gandhiji, who was from Gujarat, which is my parent's native land. I am inspired by Gandhiji, and I would like to be kind and helpful to everyone just like him.

I speak English and Gujarati and understand Spanish and Hindi. I am left-handed, and I think and act creatively. My sister and I are the only lefties in our family. I am very good at skating and swimming and playing the piano.

I like to travel to different places like the beach and enjoy the waves and sand. I want to be an inventor in the future. I enjoy playing with my friends.

My family is crazy, fun-loving, and caring. Every Friday night, we enjoy watching kid's movies. **I am very lucky and thankful for everything that I have.**

My family :)

PRINCESS AASHKA

My name is **Aashka Patel**, and I was born on May 22, 2016. My favorite things are vacations, shopping, ballet, gymnastics, swimming, writing, and arts and crafts. I love to be outdoors and play with my friends. I also love kittens and stuffed animals. My favorite colors are pink, purple, and teal. I spend a lot of time with my grandparents. I make them play silly games like robot grandma and robot grandpa and make them scare the tickle-monster (my aunt). I love my mommy very much as she loves and cares so much for me. I hope to take care of my mommy just the same when I become a big girl.

I love to wear dresses. My family has always treated me as a princess from the day I was born. **My favorite Disney princesses are Rapunzel, Ariel, Belle, Cinderella, Sleeping Beauty, Elsa, and Anna.**

Adorable ... Ambitious ... Sweet ... Happy ... Kind ... Adventurous

ME AND MY AMAZING CULTURE

Hi!! I am **Aashna**, and I am seven-and-a-half years old. Do you want to know what grade I'm in? Well, I'm in second grade. While you are reading this story, you will be able to know a lot about me and my culture. My culture is Indian American because my parents were born in India, and I was born in North America (Connecticut, USA).

There are lots of Indian festivals in India. In my opinion, my favorite is Holi! It is a festival of colors. The things we do in Holi are put colored powder on each other, and we eat delicious food like "Gujiyas." In America, you can call them "sweet pastries," but "Gujiyas" are filled with special ingredients. The other Indian festivals are Lohori, Raksha Bandhan, Navratri, and Diwali. And do you know there is a day when kids can fast? Well, there is! It is called Janmashtami.

There is something super cool about my family. My great-grandfather was a freedom fighter and my grandfather is a veteran. I feel very proud about it. Remember, I am Indian American, so I still celebrate Christmas, Easter, and the other stuff because all celebrations are fun.

Do you want me to tell you more about myself? Well, let's hop to it. My favorite color is pink. I'm really good at gymnastics, math, and reading. Writing is my jam, too. Also, some things I like to do with my family are dance to some songs when my parents pretend to be my audience, ride bikes with my parents, and most importantly, I love to cuddle and snuggle with them. **So that's the story about me and my culture.**

This is my picture! My mom took this when I was writing this story, so right now you guys are looking at the picture of the author, AASHNA GUPTA

I AM ME!

Hello! My name is **Abeer** and I am soon to be six years old.

I am funny and love to crack jokes. Sometimes I like to be silly and mess things up, too. I am smart and intelligent. Reading books is my favorite hobby.

I live with my parents; they are amazing. I love to play games with my dad and do silly things with my mom. I am their sunshine. I have a big family in India with grandparents and three cute little cousins.

Do you know that they celebrate different kinds of festivals in India? Diwali is a festival of lights, kind of like Christmas. My favorite is Holi. It's so much fun with water guns, balloons, and colors.

Do you know what the best things are in the whole wide world? It's playing with babies, eating chocolates, and driving cars. I can't wait to be a grown-up and drive my own car.

Being a kid is fun too.

I am wonderful.

I am precious.

I am me.

This is me dressed as a chef when my dad and I were preparing dinner on a friday night!

Abem Esayas

I AM ME PROJECT

My name is **Abem**. My mom calls me Abu. I was born at Saint Francis Hospital in Connecticut. I like to read and play chess and sports. I am kind and loving. Every Friday night, we have a family movie night and sleep on a mattress on the floor. That makes my family and me special, and we love doing it. My family's personalities are kind, tough, helpful, and loving. The best thing about my family is that we are always cheerful, happy, and try to look on the bright side. My name Abem means God's gift in the Ethiopian culture language. I have one older brother whose name is Nebeyu, and we are a family of four. My brother and I hope to accomplish getting good grades and helping the poor. One of my family traditions is gathering around at my aunt's house to celebrate Thanksgiving. Every summer, we call our cousins and relatives and get together on a camping trip and have fun. I love having fun with my family and friends. I am caring and a helper for my family.

Something that's passed down from generation to generation from our family is a cane from my great-grandfather, and it is over 100 years old! Something that is needed and supported by our family is always being creative, smart, and loving. Our family goes to a church every Sunday because we need to pray to God.

My parents originally came from Ethiopia. A fact about Ethiopia is that it has over eighty different languages. Another fact about Ethiopia is that it was the only country in Africa never to have been colonized, and it's the birthplace of coffee. We make a food called enjera, and it is a special food to our family, ancestors, and religion. **Here are some pictures of my family and me :)**

This is a picture of me and my family wearing clothing from our culture. We are outside for my parent's twelve year anniversary.

MY FAMILY AND ME: ALWAYS THINK INNOVATIVELY

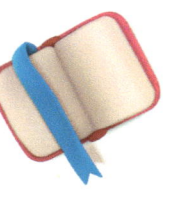

Abhinav Sai Nune

My name is Abhinav Sai. Everyone picked my first name's four letters ABHI. I live with my mom and my dad and my little sister. Her name is Aadhya.

My family identifies as Asian and we respect all cultures. We love family and relatives. In India, there are many practiced religions with many official languages. I learned the Telugu language. My grandparents live in South India. We celebrate the festivals Diwali, Holi, and Dussehra. My mom used to make traditional sweets. I love to read books and cook. In school, I am learning the violin. I used to play soccer with friends in our neighborhood.

My family enjoys spending time together. I play with my sweet little sister, and we eat dinner and watch movies on weekends together whenever possible. **I love my family. I like my school and the teachers are the best!**

This was the time when Diwali happened, which I drew.

Abhisek Harish

ABHISEK'S HISTORY AND INTERESTS

My name is Abhisek Harish. I am nine years old. I was born in India and moved to the USA in 2014. My father's name is Harish and my mother's name is Sethu Lakshmi. I have a younger brother, Tharun Sai Harish, and he is three years old. My family is supportive of each other and loves each other. We celebrate Indian festivals at home. We have a rich heritage and culture in the state I was born.

I love playing drums, and I am learning it from Mr. Gus. I can play two songs and rhymes. I am also learning Taekwondo and have a high yellow belt. I enjoy playing in the water and visiting water parks to cool myself.

I like to play and watch cricket and tennis. I also want to learn tennis and baseball and become a big player. I love to ride my bike and scooter. I spend a lot of time with my dad and brother and like to play with them outdoors.

I go to Pleasant Valley Elementary school and am in third grade. I love my school and my classmates. **All my teachers are very caring and help me learn and grow.**

Me and my brother.

I AM ADITYA

I am Aditya Pattnaik, and I am eight years old. I am in second grade. I live with my parents and my older sister Abhipsa. My first name, Aditya, means sun. I love to play outside with my friends. My favorite sport is soccer. My favorite soccer player is Cristiano Ronaldo. I love to go to school and see my friends. My family is unique because we celebrate our festivals together with our family and friends. We have many festivals like Holi (festival of colors), Diwali (festival of lights), and many more. My favorite holidays are Christmas and Halloween. My favorite subject is science because we learn new and fun things all the time. My second favorite subject is math because I love to learn math strategies.

In my free time at home, I love to draw and paint. I like to play board games like chess with my sister and my dad. I help my mom with household chores. My sister and I play hide and seek and laser tag at home. I love to play on the playscape and swing in our community playground. Some games we play on the playground are lava tag, throw ball, and catch, and I always love to win. When I lose, I become sad. I love to play video games like Spiderman and Star Wars on the PS4. I love to talk to my grandparents on the weekends on FaceTime, and I talk to my cousins, too. My mom makes me do math and my homework from school. I love to eat sweets that my mom makes for my family on various occasions. I am kind and helpful to others. My fear is bees; they scare me.

I am grateful for everything. **I love my family and friends.**

Aditya Pattnaik

This is me when I visited the Science Center in Hartford with my family.

My family is special because they are Indian, and my parents are both doctors. **Some of the fun things we do together are board games, vacations, eating out, sports, and cuddling.**

ALL ABOUT ME

My name is Aditya. People call me Adi for short. **My name means "ray of sunshine."** I live with my mom, dad, and sister. When I see them, I feel silly, nice, and loving. My family is loving, silly, and fun. My birthday is on July 25th. I was born in the year 2014. When I grow up, I want my kids to be respectful and neat. I want to make my kids learn about Indian holidays. Some Indian holidays my family celebrates are Diwali, Ganesh Chaturthi, and Holi. On these holidays we do fireworks, give presents, and we throw colors. We also make a baby Ganesh out of clay. I like Lego sets, dinosaurs, superheroes, and comics. I love my mom, chocolate, TV, new toys, and my birthday. My favorite food that my mom and dad make is kathi rolls, idli, chapati, okra, egg curry, and tindora.

Aditya – ray of sunshine

I LOVE MY FAMILY

My name is Advaith Karthik Jayanthi, and I am six years old. **My parents picked my first name, which means unique and the only one.**

I live in South Windsor, CT, with my mom, my dad, and my younger sister, Dhrithi.

I love my sister and she is my best friend. She observes and learns a lot of things from me. I try to teach her all the good things I know.

I love exploring planets and outer space. One day, when I become an astronaut, I want to take my family to Jupiter, as it is my favorite planet.

Our family is from the southern part of India, a place called Hyderabad. We have a big family back in India with many aunts, uncles, cousins, grandparents and three great-grandmothers. I love to visit my family back in India. All of us get together when we are in India and have lots of fun.

They all tell me stories and play with me whenever I am in India, and we also play games over video call when I am back in America.

As a family, we love to celebrate all our Indian festivals. We dress up in our traditional attire and cook authentic Indian food, which is unique and special for each festival. My favorite is Gulab Jamun, a traditional Indian dessert.

Out of all the festivals, Diwali and Holi are my favorite ones. During Diwali, we decorate our house with lights and oil lamps. My sister and I help our parents decorate the house and cook yummy, special food that day. We end the day with lots of fireworks.

For Holi, we put colors on our friends and family wishing them Happy Holi! We sing, dance, and eat yummy food after. It is a fun festival.

The best thing about my family is that we all work together. I love my family.

Here are pictures of my sister and me during Diwali and Holi. In the first picture, I am teaching my sister how to take photos. In the center picture, my cousins and I are having fun in India.

Adyan Malwat

Me and my brother vs. Dad.

THIS IS ME

Hi! My name is Adyan Malwat. I was born in Michigan. I live with my parents, grandparents, and my younger brother, who is very naughty. I am in first grade at Pleasant Valley School in South Windsor, Connecticut. I like to play with Legos, and I love playing soccer and basketball. I enjoy going to school and playing with my brother and my friends. I like playing outdoors.

I am learning Taekwondo, and I have achieved a high blue belt already. I will be learning to swim this summer. I LOVE water. I would stay in the water all day if I could. I am very caring and polite, and my teacher says I am the best student.

My family is from India and I have visited India twice so far. I like to learn different languages and I would love to travel. I have made a bucket list of my travel destinations, which includes California, Arizona, Florida, Canada, Australia, and London.

I always look forward to weekends because it's movie night with popcorn. I watch movies with my brother and family. **I like being with my family. Wait, what day is it? Friday? Yay, movie night. Gotta go.**

I AM ALEX

Hi, my name is Alex Beaudoin. I was born on May 7, 2014. This is a story about me and all the things I love.

I have a twin brother named Michael. I was born about one minute and twenty-one seconds after him, so I am the youngest. Michael is a great brother. We may not always get along, but I love that he is my brother. We get to play video games together and are lucky to have the same friends, too! I also have an older sister named Emilee. She is married to Scott, and they have a little boy named Harris. I am his uncle!

My dad is pretty cool. I like to hang out with him. He teaches me things like karate and cooking. We have boys' nights and watch movies, light the fireplace, make s'mores, and tell funny jokes. My mom takes great care of our family and always plans fun trips, vacations, and activities for us. She makes me feel special and loved. She is teaching me to speak Greek and learn about our Greek culture and traditions.

One of my favorite traditions is making "vasilopita," a special Greek cake for New Years. A coin is hidden inside, and the person whose slice has the coin gets good luck all year long. Someday, I hope we can visit Greece and learn more about my family and meet my many other cousins that live there.

Alexander Beaudoin

I have the sweetest dog named Sparky, whom I love so much. He is very soft, and I love to cuddle with him. Our cat, Goldie, is pretty sweet, too!

I am in second grade at Pleasant Valley School.

I enjoy playing basketball, making art, and playing video games, especially Minecraft.

Mostly, I love being seven!

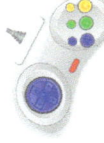

This is me. My mom took this picture one day while we were at the park having fun!

Ana Vazquez

THEY CALL ME JUJU

My name is Ana. My family calls me Juju. My late grandmother Lela gave me my nickname. She gave me the nickname Juju because my middle name is Justa, and it has Ju in the beginning, and J-u-j-u is how to spell my nickname.

I am active. I go to Muay Thai class. I know how to count to five in Thai.

I have a brother and a sister. Their names are Adrienne and Adam. I am the oldest. I chose their nicknames to match the pattern of my nickname. Adrienne's nickname is Mumu, and Adam's nickname is Bubu.

I am Puerto Rican. I love my family. I have two weekly traditions with my family. One tradition is Friday Night Dinner at my grandfather's house. I call him Papa. Papa cooks rice and beans, pernil, and tostones. Sometimes he makes spaghetti and meatballs, too. My grandmother, whom I call Mima, comes over to spend time with us.

The second weekly tradition is Saturday Movie Night with my mom, dad, and siblings. We pick a movie to watch together. I get snacks ready with my dad. These traditions are special to my family and me. **I want to keep doing these traditions when I have kids.**

This is a picture of me.

I AM ME: "PRECIOUS"

I am Amulya, born on August 15, 2013, which is Indian Independence Day. I'm very creative, and I love to draw. My name means precious and independent-born leader headed for success. My family calls me "Ammu." I am really active, but sometimes I like to stay calm. Most of the time, I do silly yoga poses inspired by animals with my friends.

I love planting seeds and plants with my dad. I also love baking and coming up with new snack recipes. I like to eat some of the Indian dishes like roti and chicken tandoori. I have learned to make roti, pizza, egg omelet, and mac-n-cheese with my mom. I have been learning to play violin since I was four years old. I am eight now, turning nine in August 2022. I love my family and friends. I have a few pet fish. I love them. I used to have a lot of fish, but some of them died. Now I have a betta fish and five goldfish. I'm very imaginative, caring, and loving. I love creating new games with my friends. My friends like playing with me and I do, too, but sometimes we have arguments, which is fine. Sometimes friends can fight and can get mad at each other, but that's okay because we will still be friends. I enjoy being in Girls Scouts and selling cookies. **I love to watch science videos, baking shows, and funny videos.**

Amulya Jyotula

Me and Agastya in ethnic wear.

I really like building with Lego blocks. Once I built an undercover science lab, and guess what it was? A cool chair that extends to the sky and spins around!

I really like playing with my friends and my brother. My brother and I like to celebrate Indian festivals like Diwali (festival of lights) and Holi (festival of colors). Our favorite holiday of the year is Christmas because we get toys. We were born to Indian parents, and the rest of my extended family lives on the other side of the world, in India, like my aunts, my uncles, my cousins, and my grandparents. I love my family because they always support and help me when I need help. As a family, we like to go on hikes and play indoor board games like Carroms, Snakes and Ladders, and chess.

My mom has two sisters, and they live in south India along with their family. My Tata (Mom's dad) was in the Indian Army a long time ago. My dad has one younger brother who lives in India as well as my grandparents. My family has taught me to be kind, helpful, caring, and sharing. Our mother tongue is "Telugu," and my family can read and write Telugu. My Amma (Dad's Mom) is a Telugu teacher. My parents are part of many charitable organizations in India.

My Little brother, called "Agastya," was born on August 8, 2016. He is in kindergarten and can hardly write. Our birthdays are one week apart, so sometimes we celebrate our birthdays together.

He is learning to play the cello. When I was three years old, I couldn't say "Agastya," so I called him "Gagu," so now all my friends and family call him "Gagu." My mom said he is named after a famous Indian Sage of Hinduism, "Agastya." He loves all colors except for pink and purple because he thinks those are girl colors. He started to read level 1 books. I like to read books to him and teach him addition. He likes beaches and outdoor activities. All my friends are his friends too, but he does not like to play with girls' dolls. He made many friends in kindergarten and still behaves like a baby sometimes. We play and fight over toys many times a day. His favorite food is vanilla ice cream and dosa (Indian pancake). We play power rangers video games together and fight sometimes. He likes to watch Blippi educational videos on TV, and his favorite is the "scoop doo" series.

We rescued a live turtle today found in our backyard.

MEET ME

Anay Mishra

On a bright, sunny July afternoon in Texas, a cute baby boy was born. My mom named me Anay, after a Hindu God, Lord Vishnu. I started my preschool in College Station, Texas, but I have faint memories of it. We moved to Connecticut when I was four years. I am eight now and a third-grader. I love my school. I have a lot of friends here, and my favorite subject is math, because I find numbers interesting. I am learning the piano. I want to become good at it, and have my own YouTube channel, and become famous.

I'm kind and respectful, which makes my parents proud. I'm sometimes shy when I meet new people, but I like to talk a lot. I like to chat with my mom and share my secrets with her. My parents are from India, but they speak two different languages. My mom speaks Assamese, and my dad speaks Hindi. I understand both their languages but can't speak them fluently. We love spending time together, and on Friday's we play board games like Scrabble and Chutes and Ladders and watch movies together. I play chess with my dad. We celebrate many festivals together. My favorite Indian festival is Diwali. I like it because it's the festival of lights. My mom decorates the house with Indian lamps and marigold flowers. I also love Christmas. It is so much fun setting up the Christmas tree and decorating with my family. I love exchanging

Decorating the Christmas tree is so much fun with my parents.

gifts too. My grandparents stay in India. I like to visit India, because I can meet them and eat yummy Indian food. My favorite foods are butter chicken and pizza.

I love to build with Lego blocks. I usually like to be creative and make my own Lego designs. I love nature as it fascinates me a lot. **When I grow up, I want to visit many places, especially Greece and Egypt, because these places have a lot of mythology and ancient history.**

Andrew (AJ) Bukowski

ALL ABOUT A.J.

On August 29, 2013, at 7:20 a.m. I came to life.
I have a sister in heaven. Her name is Katherine. She is my angel.

Nicknames were important to my mom. She wanted people to call me A.J. It stands for Andrew Jacob. I am eight years old.

Did you know my favorite animals are sharks, cats, and goldfish?

Reading, math, football, and learning about history are some of my favorite things. I really like to learn about 9/11 and the Titanic.

Everyone in my family is kind and funny. In my family, there is my mom, dad, Samantha, and my cat Charlie.

We speak Polish. We do a special blessing at Christmas; it is called Breaking the Oplatek. **It is where we break bread and wish everyone a Merry Christmas and a happy, healthy New Year.**

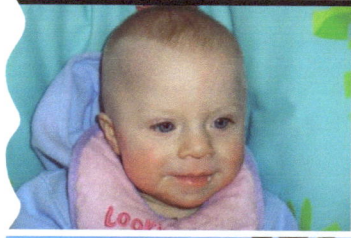

There are six pictures. A.J. playing football and soccer. One with his cat, sister, Mom, and Dad.

LITTLE MOMENTS, BIG MEMORIES

Anvi Panat

Hi, I am Anvi. I am ten years old. My family is made up of me, my mom, and my dad. I am four feet, three inches. I was born on March 8, Women's Day. Fun Fact: According to my family, I was born on Holi, a festival celebrated in India. That means that I have a second birthday and my favorite festival is also Holi. All of my relatives live in India. My other family members live in the Netherlands and Australia. I love India! I can speak and understand four languages: Hindi, Marathi (my native language), English, and a little bit of Spanish. I am learning how to read and write in Marathi. Hindi and Marathi writing looks exactly the same, but the way you say it is different. I really love to go to India, but it has been a long time since I have been there. I used to go and get sweets and treats from shops with my grandpa. I like to talk to my relatives on video calls; this way, I can stay connected and get to know them. During COVID, we even played games on video calls. I like music, and I am learning Indian classical singing. I love to read lots of long chapter books. I have read almost every single book in my room! I like to reread some of my books multiple times. If you read this in the future, you should know that the time during COVID was very

My self-portrait.

bad and boring, but I am glad to have my friends and family with me. We got through it together. **I am Anvi, and I am here to say bye and thank you for reading.**

Anya Premkumar

ALL ABOUT ME

My name is Anya and my family calls me Ani-Banani. I live with my mommy, daddy, and brother Adi. My family loves to laugh together. I love to watch movies with my family. We saw "Bunty Aur Babli" together, and it was fun. I love visiting my grandparents. My daddy's parents live in Florida, and I call them Thatha and Pati. My mommy's parents live in New Jersey, and I call them Thatha and Ammamma. I love cooking food with my family. I roll out chappati with my mommy and flip them on the stove. I wash the blueberries and make the pancake batter with my daddy; my favorite part is mixing the batter. We celebrate Christmas, Diwali, Holi, Ganesh Chaturthi, Easter, and St. Patrick's Day. Although we are Indian, we love to celebrate all holidays. I also like to dance. I am learning how to do ballet, and my mom learned Indian dancing when she was a kid. Sometimes we like to mix both types of dancing and dance together. **Our motto is "Do what makes you happy, not what others are doing, just to be the same."**

I am cutting beans with my mommy for dinner.

SINCERELY, ARIANNA

My name is Arianna Wilson, and I am a third-grader at Pleasant Valley School in South Windsor, Connecticut. I have two halves of my family; my mom's side is Italian and white, and my dad's side is African American. My birthday is on Star Wars day; "May the 4th be with you." I have dark brown hair, brown eyes, and light brown skin.

My Italian side makes a cookie called "pizzelle." They are anise-flavored, round, and have a flower pattern. Gramma Kay still has the pizzelle iron from the 1950s that Mama Toce used to bake with. I see this side of my family a lot, and we like to play board games and go to the beach. I have an older brother Cameron and a dog named Rojo.

On my African American side, Gramma Loretta likes to style my hair in pretty braids. When spending time with this side of my family, I goof around with my cousins and hang out at our grandparent's pool. I have a younger sister Alyviah who is just as silly as me.

My zodiac sign is Taurus, my favorite color is turquoise, and I'm an artist. In kindergarten, I won the "Artist of the Week" award, and in second grade, my work was featured in the town art show. A couple of my hobbies are singing in the shower, dancing, and fooling around. I love to doodle and let the creativity flow through my body. I like horse camp, and I'm a Girl Scout. This is my last year as a Brownie, and I'm excited to be a Junior next year.

Something unique about me is when I'm on a car ride on a nice day, I like to stick my head out the window while the air blows onto my face. My mom always jokes and says I'm part puppy dog; I always laugh when she says that. **I Am Me. Sincerely, Arianna**

These are a few pictures of me as a baby, me being silly, my dog Rojo, and me with my pretty braids.

Arnav Malpure

I AM ARNAV

On June 6, 2011 Arnav Malpure was born. Manchester was the city that I was born in. I grew up in Manchester and went to International Magnet School (IMS). When I turned six, my family and I moved to South Windsor. I started going to Pleasant Valley Elementary School in third grade. My family is from Maharashtra, India. We speak Marathi at home. Some things that my family likes to do together are play board games, watch TV after dinner, and celebrate festivals. Some festivals my family celebrates are Diwali, Holi, Ganesh Chaturthi, and Raksha Bandhan. My mom makes different types of food for these festivals. We celebrate Diwali with fireworks in our community. We celebrate Holi by throwing colors and spraying each other. My family makes decorations for Ganesh Chaturti. On Raksha Bandhan, my sister ties a Rakhi (cotton bracelet) around my hand. Some of my family's favorite games are Ticket To Ride, Clue, and Monopoly. Three words that I would use to describe my family would be funny, supportive, and kind. **Overall, I love my family.**

This is last year's Ganesh decoration. My family made a lotus out of paper and put it in a little tub so it looked like a lotus in a pond.

MY JOURNEY SO FAR....

Arya Bekal

My name in Sanskrit means noble and peace-loving, which I am. I am creative and can make beautiful drawings and 3D paper Airplane models, and I can build almost any Lego structure with Lego blocks and many more. I speak two languages, English and Kannada; Kannada being my mother tongue. I am not good at playing violent video games, and I sometimes feel sad about it, but my parents say it is absolutely fine and it is who I am, and they don't want me to change. I love to land and take off different aircraft on various runways on Microsoft Flight Simulator and also play chess with my grandfather. I love to bake cakes with my mom and friends, which I do during my holidays. I love music, and I am a Grade One Certified Keyboard player and also make my music on the keyboard and sing too. I love winter, the snow (the snowball fights and sledding), and all the fun I can have during the holidays. I was awarded the Dove Award in Robertson School when I was in Kindergarten as I was/am always against bullying and fighting.

I love airplanes, and my dream and ambition are to become a commercial pilot when I grow up and not a fighter pilot since I don't like fighting and wars. I want to excel in my studies, get a scholarship to college, and become the best commercial pilot. Once I earn four stripes and become a Captain of an Airliner, I will take my parents on a world tour in first class. I love my parents and could never imagine a world without them and their caring. I love my dad as he is the coolest and never says 'No' to me. My mom is sometimes strict, and she gets angry when I do some silly things and don't follow the rules she has set at home. I get sad when she is angry, but she is the best. I realized how much I

missed her when my dad and I were stuck for three months at my grandparents during COVID lockdown in India, and I missed her hugs a lot during those months. I love my cousins as I get to have a lot of fun with them. I am a proud Indian and love the rich culture and festivals celebrated all through the year. Diwali is my favorite festival as I get to fire the crackers with three days of holidays from school. I wish there would be no wars and fighting in the whole world and everyone is friends, and all the kids around the world are happy like we are with our friends and family learning and playing every day. **I wish peace and happiness to all.**

My drawings & Dove Award

Ashwin Tandon

This is me, "Ashwin," with my brother, "Shriansh." This picture was captured at Fox Hill Tower when we climbed the tree.

I AM ASHWIN

A	Amazing
S	Smart
H	Hilarious
w	Wise
I	Intelligent
N	Naughty

My name is Ashwin. I am six years old. My favorite colors are red, gold, silver, blue, and green. I like to do art because I am a great artist. I also like music; I play the piano. I know addition, subtraction, and multiplication. I like dinosaurs and turtles. I am flexible because I do gymnastic tricks. I have a pet cockatiel named Neo. He likes to eat cookies and potato chips. I have an older brother who is ten years old. His name is Shriansh. I like to play tennis. I am really smart and intelligent. I have a Tesla Model 3 that has games I can play. My favorite types of movies are comedy. I like to play Mario on my Nintendo because I win every race. **I want to be an art teacher when I grow up. I am in Mrs. Janis' class in first grade.**

THIS IS ME

I am Ayaan, and my family and friends call me "Ayu." I am a very happy-go-lucky fella. The thing that I like to do most is play.

My world is my family; my mom, papa, and my baby sister, who I love the most.

Both of my grandparents live in India. I miss them a lot. They visit me every year in the summer.

In the summer I love going to the beach.

I like playing board games.

I love pancakes. Every Sunday, I help my mom make pancakes.

Do you know about Diwali? It's my favorite festival. We do fireworks and wear new clothes and greet all our near and dear ones.

Halloween is my second favorite festival. I love dressing up for Halloween in different costumes each year.

I will be going to first grade next year, and I am very excited to turn six in August. I am going to invite my friends and celebrate it with them.

I love going to my school every day.

My teacher is the best.

The two things I like to do most; going to the petting zoo and feeding the animals, and going to the best place in the world, the amusement park. I love going to Six flags and enjoy the roller coaster rides.

Bowen Tang

How many of me can you find in this picture?

I AM BOWEN

你好, (Ni Hao), (*Hello in Chinese*), my name is Bowen Tang (汤博文). **My dad likes to call me bow-gu-la-ta because he is very silly.** My mom likes to call me Mr. B. I have a twin sister Tingya. She was born first, but now I'm much taller than her, and I have already lost four baby teeth while she's still waiting to lose her first one. We were born in Manchester, CT, in 2016.

I like to eat ice cream, to talk, to paint, and to kill bugs for my sister. I like to play outside, but I do NOT like the gym class.

My dad is like an Earth Giant to me because he is very hard working and protects the whole family all the time. My mom is like a kiss monster because she loves Tingya and me SO, SO much. As a family, we enjoy doing things together. We like to bike together, do yard work together, and decorate around the house when seasons changes and for holidays.

I have a fantabulous family.

I'm a girly girl, but I'm also a sporty girl. I like to be both!

SPORTY SPORTY, GIRLY GIRLY

My name is Braelyn.

I'm a girly girl. But I'm also a sporty girl.

I like wearing fancy jewelry,

but I also like wearing tough shin guards.

I like to do cartwheels and gymnastics tricks,

but I also like to do hard soccer kicks.

I like to be colorful and fashionable,

but I also like my gray baseball uniform.

I like to get my nails painted,

but I also like to slide into home base.

I like to wear my hair in cute styles,

but I also like to wear my baseball helmet.

I may be a girly girl, but I am also a sporty girl.

I like to be both, and I like me, just the way I am!

Camilla Baseel

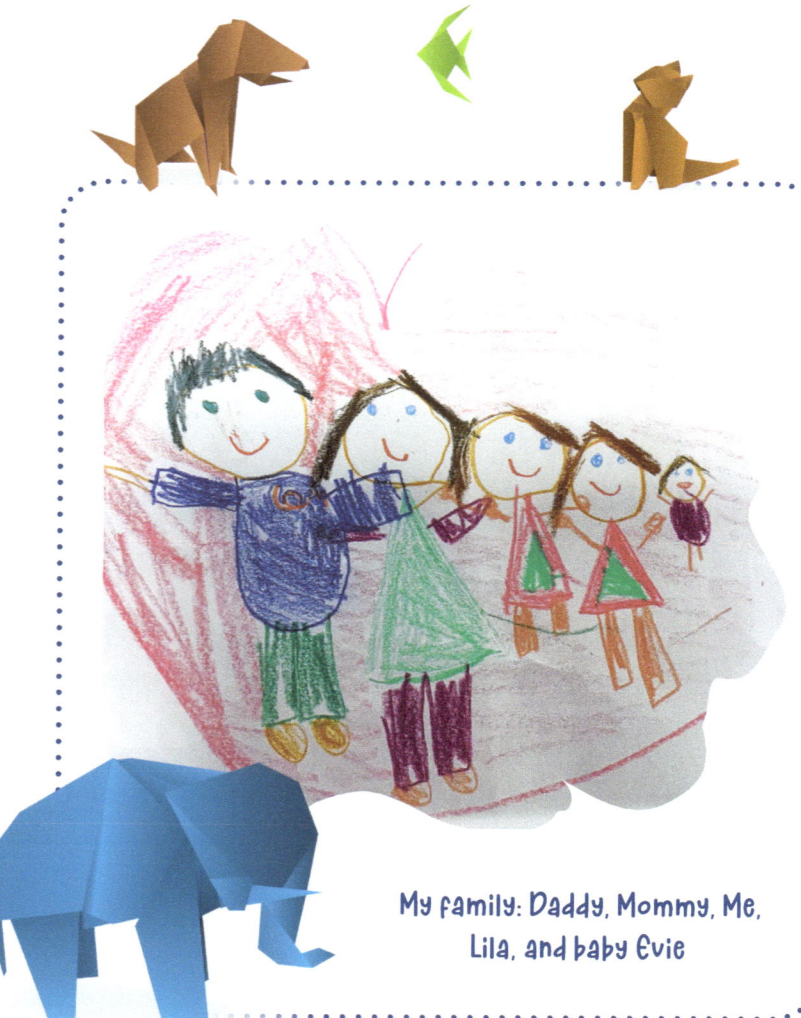

My family: Daddy, Mommy, Me, Lila, and baby Evie

WHO IS CAMILLABEAN?

One hundred and fifty years ago, I was not alive. I came into the world on September 1, 2016; I was small. My eyes are blue like Elsa's dress. My name is Camilla Randoph Baseel, but you can call me Millie. I am creative because I make little animals out of paper. My favorite color is gold because it is shiny and yellowy. I have fancy dresses that make me look and feel like I live in a wonderland. In the library, I read about life, puppies, and kitties. I like to help people when they are hurt.

I love learning about how things work; one day, I will be a veterinarian or surgeon. I go to Pleasant Valley Elementary School, where I love to play on the playscape. The spiderweb is my favorite, and I like to sit at the tippy top. I love to say "I dunno," even though I do. Cakes, cookies, and pasta noodles are my favorite things to eat. I daydream about Disneyland, New York, and South Carolina. One day I will go there.

My family is made of kind people. My daddy gives the best blanket rides, and Mommy bakes with me. Lila, my younger sister, makes me laugh with her funny questions, and Yvette, my baby sister, makes me feel secure. My uncle has pretty pictures on his arms. My Omi loves us, and my Imme cares for me. I am German, Irish, and Lebanese. I am beautiful on the inside, because I share and care. My family helps make me, me. **I am Camilla, Millie, Mills, Camillabean, Millicus. I am me.**

WHO WILL I BE?

I am Cassie Lee, a six-year-old, firstgrader at Pleasant Valley.

My Chinese nickname 开心, (Kāi Xīn) means being happy.

Being happy is being who you want to be when you grow up.

I conducted interviews and first asked my grandpop,

"What do you want to be when you grow up?"

"A grandpa!" laughed Pop.

My 爷爷 (Yé Yé, grandfather in Chinese) said happily,

"A chef, cooking for my family!"

Then I turned to Mommy and Daddy,

"When you were a child, what did you want to grow up to be?"

Mommy smiled, "A working writer!"

Daddy jumped in, "A world traveler!"

When it was my brother's turn to share,

"A bat, a wolf, and a cheetah!" Caden was eager to declare.

Joined our family cat Mochi,

"Meow wants to play, eat, and sleep." She purred at me.

I asked everyone, as I stood tall.

"Have you become who you want to be or not at all?"

I collected five "Yeses."

Guess who reached their successes?

Then my loving, artistic, and kind family asked me,

My Very First
Hand-sewn Pillow!

"Cassie, when you grow up, what will you be?"

"A teacher, a designer, a librarian, a mom, and a sewist!"

My list could go on, to be honest.

And the secret to being who you want to be when you grow up?

Stay focused, keep practicing, and never give up!

Chase Kulpa

Swimming at my Memere & Pepere's pool!

I AM CHASE!

I am Chase Scott Kulpa.

I am named after my Papa.

I am six years old.

I am athletic. I love playing baseball.

I am kind, especially when playing with my younger cousin Mason.

I am most excited to play with my friends.

I am excited to learn about numbers; I love when my teacher teaches me math!

I am someone who loves the beach; I go on vacation every year to Cape Cod with my mommy and daddy.

I am loving and love when my Memere gives me big hugs.

I am a comedian; I like to make people laugh.

I am brave but sometimes get nervous.

I am creative.

I am a hard worker.

I am adventurous. My mommy says I give her gray hair.

I am caring.

This is me, I AM CHASE SCOTT KULPA.

I AM COLIN

Hi! My name is Colin Francis Gagnon.

My middle name is from my Pepe, which is what I call my grandfather on my father's side.

My grandfather on my mother's side is my Appachi. My family says I look a lot like my Appachi when he was little.

My grandmothers are my Meme on my dad's side and Ammachi on my mom's.

My family is unique because we are mixed.

My mother's side is Indian. My father's side is mainly French Canadian, but also a little Irish and Italian.

When I visit my Ammachi she makes us chapatis with chicken curry. These are yummy!

When I visit Meme she lets us do crafts in her craft room.

I enjoy playing sports, video games, and playing with my friends and family.

My favorite sport is baseball. I got my love of baseball from my dad, who played baseball his whole life. He is now coaching my Majors baseball team. We are the White Sox.

My dad got his love for baseball from my Pepe. Baseball is important in my family. It is important to me to carry on my love of baseball to my kids and grandkids someday.

As a family, my parents and sister and I like to take vacations together. My favorite vacation so far was when we went to Disneyland in California last summer. We also like to watch TV together, and right now, we are watching Cobra Kai.

I feel special being part of this family and being myself.

My family and me after my first Holy Communion. I'm the boy in the center.

Daniel Guarnieri

This is me with one of our chicks, Rosie.

I AM DANIEL

My name is Daniel Salvatore Guarnieri and I love to read! I like to play with my yo-yo, my legos, and my pokemon cards. I also LOVE to play outside. My favorite outside activities are riding my skateboard and my bike. My dad taught me how to ride both my skateboard and my bike. My dad is the only person who calls me by my nickname, Danny.

My dad is only one part of my family. My mom is also part of my family. She is a great cook and my favorite food that she makes is ... EVERYTHING! Faith is my two-year-old sister. She is finally big enough to swing on our playscape, and I usually push her. I LOVE playing outside with her. Saiorse is my four-year-old sister, and I like to build forts together with her. Sometimes they are really big. In our family we also have two cats, one fish, one frog, and six chicks! My favorite tradition with my family is Thanksgiving. We have to use two tables because we invite so many family members! It is a lot of fun!

I am Daniel. And I love being part of my family!

MY WORLD

Dhruv Ganesh

I am Dhruv Ganesh.

My parents, little brother, and grandparents complete my world, which is full of fun and joy. I exactly predicted the day when my little brother would enter our lives. My family was thrilled.

I am passionate about reading books. Books are funny and entertaining. They transport me to different worlds. Books make me feel joyful. I am overjoyed when I read to my little brother and teach him new words. Words make me feel curious. I have started learning different languages at home and school.

I love making art projects. A few of my drawings have been awarded International-level accolades. I often create my own toys and games using recyclable products available at home, such as cereal and butter boxes. I transform every blank piece of paper/sheet at home into something colorful.

I love to play games with my family, and we enjoy eating together every day. Gulab Jamun, Kaju Katli, Mysore Pak, and Chana Masala are a few all-time favorite sweets that my mother makes. I love cooking too. I enjoy baking cupcakes with banana and chocolate chips.

I like to sing. While traveling, we listen to recordings of my songs. We also love singing together. Sometimes, we take turns and quiz each other.

I love my school. My teachers teach me new things. I enjoy playing with my friends. I have been greatly appreciated for following my school's expectations and showing responsibility.

I care for my society. I use electricity and water carefully.

Before I sleep, my parents tell me stories. I fall asleep dreaming of wonderful discoveries and adventures. This is the favorite part of my day.

I dream of becoming a scientist, inventing medicines, and serving my society.

My painting of my school mascot "Popcorn," protecting endangered species, and my very own Candyland filled with all my favorite foods.

Diya Ayanikkat

I LOVE "ONAM!"

Hello! My name is Diya Ayanikkat. My family calls me Chinnu. My parents are from India. My grandparents live in India, too. I was born in Hartford, Connecticut. When I was born, I was only four pounds, so my parents had to wait a few more days to take me home. I live in South Windsor.

I love to draw, color, sing, and dance. I like to draw animals the most. My favorite song is "Easy on Me," by Adele. When I got a chance, I used to record myself singing and put it on YouTube. Then I'd share it with my grandparents and aunts.

My family celebrates "Onam" every August/September. It's the harvest festival of South India. We have our feast with our family. We make "flower rangoli" (patterns with flowers) in front of our house. We wear traditional Indian dresses during the celebration. We prepare lots of delicious sweets. Our friends and family get together on that day. Ladies will perform a traditional dance called "Thiruvathira."

I always look forward to celebrating Onam with my family. This summer, we're going to India to see my grandparents. **I can't wait to have lots of fun and enjoy Onam with them.**

This is me wearing a traditional South Indian dress. My mom took this picture last year on Onam.

I took this picture when I first figured out I wanted to start doing photography.

Eden Hauschild

I AM EDEN

I am Eden. I love to play basketball, and I love drawing. My favorite colors are mint green and pastel yellow. My favorite specials are art and gym. My zodiac sign is a Pisces which is the zodiac of the fish. I am half Cuban and half American. I have straight, brown hair and brown eyes. I am part of a family of four: me, my younger sister Leila, my mom, and my dad. Over spring break, my family and I went to Hershey Park. We had almost as much chocolate as we did fun. My favorite foods are burgers and Chinese food. My lucky numbers are 11 and 21. My name (Eden) means paradise, like the garden of Eden. Another hobby I have is photography; most of the time I take pictures in the air. I like taking outdoor pictures in the grass or on my deck. I also love all things Harry Potter. My Hogwarts house is Gryffindor, and my Patronus is a horse which makes sense because I love horses! Speaking of Harry Potter, I am currently reading the third Harry Potter book.
That is me, and I am Eden.

Elena Claire Proano

THIS IS ME

My friends call me Ellie, but my real name is Elena. I am nine years old. I see myself as smart, athletic, and kind. I do tap dancing and ballet. I compete in tap dancing with a group of friends. We have won lots of awards. I also play soccer. I like to write stories that sometimes just pop into my head, and I want to publish them. I also like to read, especially Harry Potter.

My mom's side of the family is Canadian, Italian, and Polish. My dad's side of the family is Colombian. That is how my family is unique. I really, really, really want to go to Colombia next summer to see my Grandma "Tita" who lives there.

My family and I love to make Arepas, a special Colombian bread that my dad sometimes makes us for breakfast. We also make a recipe for "everything cheeseburgers," where we mix a bunch of things in the meat like cheese, vegetables, and bacon. Over summer break, we like to go camping, travel, and go in the pool!

I have a kitty named Tippy. He can sometimes get into a lot of trouble, but he is also good to snuggle with.

That is me, and I am special!

This is me getting ready for a dance competition. I have makeup on and my team jacket.

EXCLUSIVELY ELI! ALL ABOUT ELI AND THE PETGRAVE FAMILY

My name is Elias, but everyone calls me Eli. I am six years old, and I am in second grade. You might be wondering how I am in second grade when I am only six years old. It is because I was only in first grade for four weeks, and then I went to second grade because I am a smart boy. My brain works a little differently because I learn things really fast. I am different because I really like to challenge myself in school. I really love football, and I want to play college football, but I am even more excited to play football in the NFL. When I grow up, and after I play football in the NFL, I want to be President of the United States.

Let me tell you about my family. My family is different in many ways. We come from different cultures and backgrounds. My mom is Italian and Lebanese, and my dad is Jamaican, and that makes me Italian, Lebanese, and Jamaican. We celebrate our cultures with food and traditions. We also have some unique family hobbies. We are beekeepers, and we sell local honey at the farmer's market. My mom also owns a cookie company. She makes the best cookies ever. Another thing that makes my family unique is that my mom adopted my older sister, Olivia. I love baking with

Here are some photos of me, Eli, and all of the things I love! I love football (and all sports), beekeeping, and my family. When I grow up, I want to play football in the NFL and then I want to be President of the United States!

my sister and my mom, and I also love playing games with them. My brother, Kyson, is eleven years old, and I love playing sports with him outside. I also really love fishing and playing video games with Kyson and my dad. My mom and dad always say how special my sister and brother and I are. They always tell us to reach for the stars and that hard work pays off. I really love my family, and I love being different.

I love being me ... Eli.

I AM EMMY

My family calls me "Emmy," but my full name is Emily. I like dinosaurs. If I could travel I would go back in time to the Jurassic Period and live in Camp Cretaceous. I want people to know that I am funny and sometimes lazy. At home, I like to watch TV, and play on my tablet, but sometimes I like to go crazy and read a book.

In my family, we have four people and one kitty. The people are Daddy, Mommy, Elena, and me! With my family, I like to play games, travel, and go to the campground. We also like to cook together, especially eggs and arepas! Arepas are a Colombian food. They are like a round bread with cheese inside, called "Arepas con queso." My dad is from Colombia, and he teaches us to make Colombian food.

My kitty's name is Tippy. He is almost two years old! We named him Tippy because he has a white tip on his tail. **He is funny when he falls off his cat post!**

This was my cat, Tippy, when he was a baby. He is a boy. He didn't have a mommy so he drank his milk from a bottle.

A FEW THINGS ABOUT ME

Hi guys! My name is Emma Sophia Breen! I am eight years old. I was born March 20, 2014. I picture myself as a "blooming flower" because my birthday is the first day of Spring.

I have four aunts. They are Aunt Leslie, Titi Sio (Rossio), Titi Nis (Denisse), and Titi Qui (Orquidea). I have three uncles (Uncle Jim, Uncle Andrew, and Uncle Dave). I have two grandmas (Grandma Joyce and Mama Maria) and two grandfathers (Grandpa Tom and Papa Hector). I have seven cousins; Sarah, Andrew, Colin, Max, Avery, David Jr. (DJ), and Henry. DJ and Henry were born last year in 2021. Avery died when I was seven years old. Other important people in my family are Nichole, Kim, Leo, Edward, and Momin.

My Dad's family came here from Ireland, Scotland, England, and Canada, and guess what? My dad even had an ancestor that came on the "Mayflower." My mom's family came here from the Dominican Republic over eighteen years ago.

What I love about my family is that we come from places all over the world. We also love traveling to places like Newport, RI (my favorite), Florida, and the Dominican Republic.

My favorite color is pink, and my favorite food is pizza. If you know me, you will notice I say the word "pizza" every day, multiple times.

My favorite holiday is Christmas, because I love giving presents, opening presents, and being with my family.

I love my family because they are helpful, funny, and tell me they love me every day!

My favorite time of the year is Christmas! I love it because it brings so much happiness, our family and friends get together, and we give and open presents together.

Eshaal Atif

I AM ESHAAL, CUTE LITTLE TALKER AND SHOPPER!

funtime with Mom

My name is Eshaal Atif, and the meaning of my name is Flower of Paradise. I was born on January 17, 2015, in Karachi, Pakistan.

I am seven years old and in grade one at Pleasant Valley Elementary School. I live with my parents and my little brother, Hashir, whom I love to tease and play with. My favorite foods are pasta, pizza, burgers, and tater tots. I enjoy painting, playing with my family, reading books to them, and talking until I sleep.

I love to visit Pakistan so I can meet my grandparents, cousins, uncles, and aunts. We can talk for hours about everything, share stories with each other, and go together for dining and shopping :). Shopping is my favorite hobby. I like to go to Walmart, shopping malls, and Claire's so I can buy new things from there. I am a fun, loving, confident girl, but sometimes I get silly. **I am a little impatient, but I am working hard on it.**

ALL ABOUT FANAR

I was born on November 26, 2012. Both of my parents are from Iraq, and they are Muslim so I am Muslim. My favorite time of year is Ramadan. This is when we fast from sunup to sunset for 30 days. At the end of Ramadan, we celebrate Eid el-Fitr. This is a time when you celebrate the end of Ramadan and eat a good meal of something we don't get to eat often.

My family is very close. I have an aunt and a grandma who live with me and another aunt and grandmother who live in Manchester. I love how all of my aunts and my grandmothers take care of me like I'm their own child. My mom and grandma are amazing cooks! They make great Arabic food. My favorite Arabic dish is moukia. It is a green leafy vegetable on top of rice, and it is delicious! My dad is an amazing cook, too. He makes the most awesome steak on the grill. His steak is always so tender and cooked perfectly (medium).

I also have two brothers, Busher and Anas. Busher is in college, and Anas is in high school. They love to go to the gym to work out.

I'm very specific in what I like to do and eat. I love to play basketball, and I really enjoy swimming. I have a pool at my house, and I swim in it almost every day in summer. In the summer I really love working in the garden and growing my own vegetables and fruits. My favorite ones to eat fresh from the garden are cucumbers, strawberries, raspberries, and cherry tomatoes.

In school, my favorite subject is science. I like to do experiments. My favorite experiment was an engineering project where we used coffee stirrers and clay to make a skyscraper that could withstand an earthquake. Ours did really well, even when we flipped it over!

When I grow up, I want to be a detective. I am really good at solving things and I want to help other people. When my aunt asks something like "Who took the last cookie?" I am really good at searching my brother's rooms and finding out who did it. **I hope that whatever I do when I grow up, I will have a career that helps people.**

This is a picture of me and my dad. My entire family is so important to me.

Fathima Nashwa Changampally Kizhakkumapttu

Me acting like the Statue of Liberty. It was really nice weather.

I AM NASHWA

On November 30, 2011, I saw the world as a baby. I am Nashwa. Since I was a little kid, I was really shy to meet new people. I much prefer the fresh air, though I don't like bugs that much. I got used to it though. I am a nature lover. On September 26, 2015, I had a sister. In 2019, on June 26th, I had another sister. She was born in Connecticut, USA. They were just like me, shy to meet new people. Siblings can be annoying, but imagine being an only child; you would have no one to play with and no one to fight with (okay I was kidding about that—we don't want anyone to fight with us). I am the oldest kid.

On March 17, 2019, I came to Connecticut, USA. It was really cold. It was my first time in America. It was my first time in the snow and things really changed after coming here. It was my first time noticing the difference between all the seasons. It was also my first time learning in an American school. It was my first time making friends in an American school. I am inexperienced. I am the religion of Islam, which means that I am unique by following another religion. I am going to wear a hijab at some point in my life, which also means that I dress differently. **I also speak a different language. I am a Muslim. I am Nashwa.**

I AM ME

Gabriel Davies

Everyone calls me Gabe, but my full name is Gabriel Jon Davies. I was named after my uncle Jon Davies. He was a Worcester, MA firefighter who died putting out a house fire. Even though he died before I was born, I love him very much, and he's my hero.

My father is Lithuanian, English, and Polish. My mother is Italian. My Nonna and Nonno were born in Italy. I cook Italian food with my Nonna. We make pizzelles and cavatelli, and I listen to her tell me stories of her growing up in Italy.

I have an older brother and sister and two dogs named Willow and Belle. My family loves to be outdoors and fish, hike, and kayak. My favorite activities are playing baseball and playing video games with my friends. I love to jump on my trampoline and swim in my pool. My favorite season is winter, and I love sledding and building snowmen.

I am Gabe Davies, and I am nine years old. I am strong and smart. **I am kind and friendly. Best of all, I am me!**

Kayaking with my dad in Maine.

Gihon Emmanuel

SCIENTIST IN THE MAKING

I am Gihon Joseph Emmanuel. I am eight years old. I go to Pleasant Valley Elementary School. I am a happy, silly boy. My parents say that I am an overcomer and filled with God's grace. My name means "Valley of grace," "Successful and Overcomer."

My parents are from India. My dad and my mom work during weekdays and are very kind to me. They both help me with my work. They help correct my mistakes. I help them in return by doing small chores at home. I like to help my mom with her vegetable garden. I have one older brother, and I call him "Anna," which means "Older Brother" in Tamil. I know another language other than English - Tamil! I have a Tamil class every Friday. Every Sunday, I go to church. I am a Christian, and I believe in one God.

My favorite drink is chocolate milk. I love mac & cheese. I like to watch videos about Bey Blade and

Gihon – exploring nature and reaping benefits.

science experiments. I love drawing, coloring, doing science experiments, and, especially, playing video games. I like playing with my pet dog Brownie. He likes my brother and me very much.

When I grow up, I want to be a scientist and help find a cure for all pandemic-causing viruses. **I envision the world to be a happy, safe, and kind place for me and everyone.**

I'M HARSHETH

It's me, Harsheth Gurumoorthy. My parents and friends call me Harshu! I'm seven years old, born two days before 4th of July on July 2nd. I'm a second grader at PV, and I love my school and teacher (Mrs.Cherko). I love to read books and play with my friends. I enjoy spending time with my baby brother Ashvith. He really likes me, and he is nine months old. He is starting to crawl.

I'm Spiderman at jumping, Iron Man at Math, Hulk at eating ice cream, Thor at riding a bike, and Captain America at art!

My favorite color is green, fruits are mango and pineapple, and animals are grizzly bear and rabbit.

My most loved festival is Diwali. We celebrate with fireworks, sweets, and yummy foods. We also invite friends. We also celebrate this south Indian festival called Pongal, connected with harvest season. **On this day, we eat this food called Pongal prepared in clay pots using sticks or logs for heating.**

At my home, chilling out, with my little brother,

Hasini Kasam

I AM HASINI

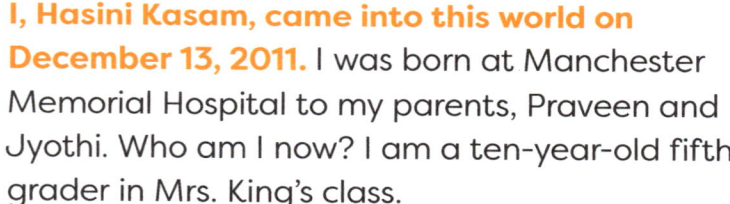

I, Hasini Kasam, came into this world on December 13, 2011. I was born at Manchester Memorial Hospital to my parents, Praveen and Jyothi. Who am I now? I am a ten-year-old fifth grader in Mrs. King's class.

I am the oldest child to my parents. I am also a sister to my cute first-grade brother, Hanish. Hanish is in Ms. Devlin's class at PV. He is crazy about Paw Patrol. We do fight a lot, but we care for each other. Our extended family is in South India, and we talk with them very frequently.

I love reading thick, chapter books about relationships and social issues because I can learn new things that connect to the real world and I can use them. I can finish a book in a few days, so I am always on the lookout for some new ones. I also like painting. Painting is a fun time-passer. I try to do my best and fix mistakes because I know it'll be worth a beautiful picture in the end. Finally, I love music. I can sing along with some of the most popular Telugu songs, and I love moving around to them too.

My favorite food is brownies, and my favorite Indian snack is Sakinalu, a crunchy hoop-shaped treat. I also like being with the neighbors' toddlers, trying to teach them new things, and playing with them. I've always wanted to get a dog or cat, so I try to earn as many opportunities as I can to hang out with them, too.

I am from Telangana state in India. I speak Telugu, unlike my friends who speak Tamil and Hindi. It feels different celebrating different holidays and naming things with different words, but it's also what makes me unique. Being from India also makes me very annoyed when somebody mispronounces an Asian name.

I am Hasini! This is what makes me special!

This is a painting I did recently by cutting up some jeans and gluing them onto the paper to make a designer outfit.

I AM ME: HENRY ADADE & FAMILY

On Sunday, June 16, 2013, the words, "Congratulations" and "Happy Father's Day" rang at St. Francis hospital. My mom delivered her first-born child, Henry Kwesi Ofosu Adade, Jr. I am named after my father. The name Kwesi Ofosu comes from the country of Ghana, West Africa, and means born on Sunday. I was happy to be a part of this world and ready for the journey. However, my mother says that the journey wasn't that easy; for nine months, she had an achy back and swollen feet, but in the end, she received a beautiful gift with big brown eyes and bushy hair.

Today, I am eight years old and in third grade at Pleasant Valley School. The most exciting thing about me is my Ghanaian culture. Every Sunday, my family eats a delicious meal called fufu, a dough-like cassava eaten with soup. On holidays, we attend my grandparents' church and sing and dance to African drums pounding while waving our handkerchiefs in the air. My dream is to go to Ghana one day so I can see my aunts and uncles. My parents have been teaching me how to speak Twi, the largest spoken language in Ghana. Now I know how to say, Ei tisen (how are you) and wo din de sɛn (what is your name). When I finally arrive in Ghana, I'll be ready.

Being an older brother can be fun and a lot of work at the same time. I have to teach my brother and sister how to ride a bike and make their bed. I also have to take the blame when something goes wrong, which isn't so fun. On Saturday mornings, I play hockey for the South Windsor Knights, and for fun, I play basketball with my uncle Jr.

I love being a part of this world, where everyone can love themselves and just be "Me."

On Sunday afternoons, I practice my martial arts moves before I head to class. Learning different ways to be "me" through movement is what I like.

Hruthi Bhavanasi

I AM HRUTHI

Hello! My name is Hruthi Anwitha Bhavanasi. I live with my cute family of my dad, my mom, and my little sister. My little sister is very naughty 😈. My sister and I are very affectionate with each other.

I am studying first grade in Pleasant Valley Elementary School. I love my teacher and my friends.

I love to play tennis 🎾. My father is my coach. My favorite festival is Diwali 🪔. On this day, our family decorates the house with so many colorful lights and enjoys the fireworks 🎆. I am from India 🇮🇳. I like America 🇺🇸.

Thank you.

My cute family 👨‍👩‍👧‍👦

MY FAMILY AND ME

My name is Isabella and I am in second grade. Most people call me Bella. I live in South Windsor with my mom, dad, sister, and our dog Mia. I have brown hair, brown eyes, and I am tall. My family comes from many different countries like Japan, Israel, Poland, and Canada. I have family all over the country in Connecticut, New York, Massachusetts, Texas, Arizona, Florida, and Washington D.C. My family likes to get together and celebrate holidays, birthdays, and special occasions together. We also like to get together for meals and to go to different places. We like to go to the beach in Rhode Island, the pool, see fireworks, take bike rides, and walks. I enjoy playing outside with my sister, friends, and neighbors on our playset, trampoline, bikes, and scooters. Some other things I enjoy are horseback riding, Girl Scouts, Ninja Challenge, swimming lessons, and gymnastics. In the summertime, my sister and I go to summer camp and do lots of different activities like riding bikes, having water day, movie day, and arts and crafts. Some of the holidays my family likes to celebrate are Christmas, Hanukkah, Easter, Halloween, and Thanksgiving. We usually go to my grandma's house for Easter and my other grandma's house for Hanukkah. My cousins come to my house for Halloween, and I go to all of their houses for Christmas. In the summer, I like to

go to the pick-n-patch down the street to pick flowers, fruits, and vegetables. **I also enjoy playing with my friends outside.**

I love rainbows, and I love when it rains and a rainbow comes.

I AM IVAN P. CHITTISSERY

I was born on March 27, 2012, in Madison, Wisconsin. I moved to Connecticut when I was one year old. I love my family, which consists of my brother and my parents. Most of my relatives are in India. I wish to have them with me in my journey of life.

When I was four years old, I went back to India along with my mom and brother for three years. I had an enjoyable time being with my grandparents and relatives, but I missed my father. The school I joined was amazing, and I learned a new language called Malayalam. I took part in all sports and drama, which helped me make more friends.

After I finished first grade in India, I came to the USA and started second grade in PV. I started missing friends and relatives back in India. When I started fourth grade, I had a good relationship with the people in my grade. This made me happier about leaving India.

In my spare time, I like to play video games with my brother and friends. My favorite sport is tennis. I also like to play tag, badminton, table tennis, chess, swimming, bowling, and biking. I have a strong passion for reading fantasy books.

My entire family calls me Tikku because it is my nickname. I like watching movies with my family. We go to church together on Sunday. If I could describe my family, I would describe them as kind, happy, and humorous.

My life had a lot in it. Going to India, family, coming back to the USA, spending time searching and doing hobbies and passions, and good education, these things are most of what made my life. **My life is happy, but sometimes there are troubles in life, but I keep moving with the wonderful journey of life!**

This is me, Ivan, in the church for my first Eucharist celebration. I was prepared for the prayers I had to say.

UNICORN GIRL

My name is Izzy. I like all the colors in the rainbow. I love unicorns because they are magic. I have a unicorn shirt, a unicorn dress, and unicorn pants. On summer break, I am going to Nonna and Papa's house. They live in Ohio. I will get to play with my cousins. I like to ride their power wheels. We get to stay at a hotel and swim in a pool. I love my two sisters and one brother. **There are six people in my family.**

This is a picture of me and a unicorn at the Roger Williams Zoo in Rhode Island.

Jackson Lydecker

I AM JACKSON

I am Jackson.

On Saturday, October 8, 2011, I was born.

When I was born, the nurses said I was the most beautiful baby they had ever seen.

When I grow up, I want to be a videogame tester.

I am good at making new friends.

I have a lot of friends.

I am funny. I can make funny jokes.

Also, I can be funny without trying to be funny.

I am a lover of books.

I live with my mom, dad, and brother.

My grandpa is named Bob, but we call him Beep.

We call my grandpa Beep because when I was little, he had a Jeep and his Jeep always went like BEEP BEEP.

I am ten years old and in fifth grade.

I have two cats.

One is named Smokey, and one is named Mia.

I am adventurous and like to ride on ziplines because they are fun.

In swimming, I earned a ribbon for my most improved time on backstroke.

I am part German, French, Canadian, Dutch, and Welsh.

I am good at video games.

My favorite video game is Bee Swarm Simulator on Roblox.

I am good at math.

I can read almost a book a day.

My favorite genres are horror, fantasy, and myth.

I like baseball and tennis.

I also like roller coasters and Harry Potter.

I like skiing and swimming.

I can do flips on the diving board.

I am good at skiing, because I got one gold medal, one silver medal, and two bronze medals.

My favorite colors are dark purple and lightish orange.

I am good at making memes in my head. (A meme is a funny thing or joke that usually has a picture with it.)

One time my mom made me a page of division problems, and I solved them faster than she thought them up.

One time I was skiing and my mom told me to turn, so I turned and skied right off the mountain. In summer, I do the swim team, and in winter, I am on RTD (Race Team Development) at Ski Sundown.

All of this makes me, me.

I am Jackson.

This is a drawing of me, Jackson.

This is me outside with my long hair and shorts.

Jacob Edwards

I AM JACOB

My name is Jacob William Edwards. I have the nickname Jake. I was born in Connecticut, but all my cousins and my dad were born in New Jersey. My middle name is after both of my great-grandfathers. I'm tall, funny, smart, and kind. I'm Irish and French Canadian. I wear shorts and a T-shirt every day and night of the year, even when it's snowy or rainy. I like to play sports like soccer. I am a goalie. I also like to play football and my position is a lineman. I love to play most sports. I'm the youngest in my entire family, including my seventeen cousins. I have a really big family. I really love to eat Cheetos and cookies. My family has a tradition of having everyone over for Thanksgiving at my aunt's house for dinner. My family is different because my ancestors are from other countries. I live with my dad, my mom, and my sister. **I have thirty members in my entire family.** Also, I am really athletic.

Jay Aditiya

THIS IS JAY

I am Jay Aditiya, and I am nine years old.
I was born in Connecticut, and I live in South Windsor with my mom, my dad, my little sister, and my dog, Bruno.

I am a proud American with ties to four countries. My grandparents live in Australia and New Zealand, and my cousins and extended family live in India. We speak English at home even though my parents speak different languages like Tamil, Malayalam, and Hindi. I celebrate American traditions and festivals, and I am also very familiar with Indian culture.

I enjoy watching music videos from all around the world with my parents every weekend that includes music from Europe, Asia, Africa, the Middle East, and the America's. We listen to music in different languages even if we don't understand!

I have been following Formula One motor racing with my dad since 2019, and I know all the teams and their drivers. I love answering trivia questions. I practice Kenpo Karate, and I love swimming, playing chess, and soccer.

I want to become an engineer and build robots when I grow up. I like hands-on activities and helping my dad with setting up gadgets and home improvement projects. I love helping my mom with planning parties.

I love hanging out with my friends, collecting Pokémon cards, playing video games, and doing creative things. I love reading books, especially at bedtime.

My grandparents live far away, on the other side of the world, but still, we connect and see each other often through video chat. I have been fortunate to travel to nine countries and the Northeast Coast of the US with my parents. **I think my family is unique as they make sure I experience different cultures, traditions, foods, and music; it makes me more aware of the world.**

Hanging out with my buddy, Bruno!

I AM ME: THE BEST I CAN BE!

Hi. My name is Jay. I'm eight years old.

I enjoy building things like circuits. You might not know what a circuit is, but that is just one of the unique things about me. I am destined to be an engineer and not a co-worker, a boss. Yeah! I'm an engineer at heart.

I love building things with Zoobs, Lego, and Snap Circuits. I created a life-sized jetpack because I can go faster than a car. I make robots, rovers, radios, and invent stuff. Now, I'm building a PyGamer and programming games for it. I bought the parts with chore money. It took a long time. I looked at the parts on Adafruit for months dreaming of it. I can't wait to use it! I play, create, build, and make.

I love to play. If I could, I would play all day, every day!

I love to read books. I really like movies, but I like books better. I like movies, because you can see the graphic image like it's real. Sometimes the special effects look real!

My favorite sport is basketball. I love dribbling down the court and making the shot that goes in! I love that feeling! I can swim for hours like a fish. I love rock climbing all the way to the top, like I'm on top of a mountain. I like to boulder in caves and love going upside down! I pretend I'm Spiderman! Thwip! Thwip!

I love to roll down the hill! I'm having a jolly good time!

My favorite foods are garlic, butter spaghetti with parmigiano reggiano and camarao com molho de vinho e alho.* My favorite dessert is ice cream.

I have two dogs, Zane and Penelope. I like to take them for walks and spend time with everyone. I'm one hundred percent American. I'm tan. **I'm me. I'm the best I can be!**

*Portuguese shrimp with wine and garlic sauce"...like mighty old England.

Jayce Marshall

I AM JAYCE ... A DEDICATED STUDENT ATHLETE

I am Jayce Marshall, and I am nine years old.

I was born eight lbs., fifteen oz, and twenty-two inches.

My parents said that I was a big baby, and I was born with a smile!

I was born to a Jamaican mother and an American father.

I have two other siblings, an older brother Justin and a younger sister Michala.

So, yes, that makes me the middle child!

I am a great student. I play the cello, but most importantly, I like to play sports.

My parents often tell me that I am a natural-born athlete!

My favorite sports are baseball and track and field, but the sport that I like the most is football.

This year I competed in a National Track and Field Championship, and I became an All-American athlete.

My favorite football position is playing wide receiver and cornerback.

I like being a wide receiver, because when the quarterback throws the ball, the wide receiver has a chance to make a touchdown.

I am a son, I am a brother, and I am a friend, but my favorite title is being a student-athlete. Playing sports has always been my passion.

I also like being a cornerback, because the cornerback guards the wide receiver. The cornerback can jump to make an interception and get a touchdown! This is called a pick-six.

I like both positions, because there is a chance to score a touchdown!

I play football in my town league, and last year in 2021, my team won the state championship.

Everyone on my team had a chance to keep the trophy for a week.

I was super excited because this experience was like winning the Super Bowl!

One day my dream is to play in the NFL as a professional football player.

I know that with hard work, one day my dream will come true!

I am Jayce Marshall and I hope that you enjoyed learning about me!

I AM KAITLYN HUBBARD

I am Kaitlyn Elizabeth Hubbard. My family and I love animals, sports, and going on vacations. I am the third out of four kids and I love having fun with my family. I do a lot of sports like ninja, figure skating, softball, and basketball. My main sport is figure skating. Figure skating is like ice skating but you do tricks. I love skating and that's why I compete!

My family and I absolutely love animals. We have seven animals at home. Max, Molly, and Lucas are our three dogs. Bella, Buttons, and Midnight are our three cats. RJ is our turtle.

My family and I love going on vacation. We go on a lot of them thanks to my mom. We've been to so many places like Hawaii, Florida, Canada, Iceland, Ecuador, and so many others. **My family is kind of crazy, but I love them.**

Kaitlyn Hubbard

This is me doing what I love!

Killian Drummond

WHO I AM

I am American, of Irish, Jamaican, African, and Scottish ancestry, from Vernon, South Windsor, Hartford, and Manchester. I am from the Wolves, Tulips, and Palm Trees. I am from Christmas, St. Patrick's Day, amazing family vacations, and arts, painting, drawing, and creativity. I am from Grammie Bet, Grammie Dorn, my Grandfather's Keith and Tom, Dad, Mom, Marcel, and Olibhia. I am from "be kind, do your best, have fun, have good morals, and I love you's." I am from Manchester, mac & cheese, steak, chicken parm, cucumbers, and mashed potatoes. I am a descendant of Pirate Queen Grace O'Malley (Grainne Ni Mhaille), who loved to travel and confronted Queen Elizabeth I. I am from the love of travel, which has been passed on to me. I am from beaches and waves and mountains the same. One day, I hope to go to Ireland, Paris, Hawaii, and Canada with my family. I am from Music, Reggae, Rap, and Rock. I am from hard work, love, patience, persistence, support, and fun. I am from being a good friend, playing video games, flag football, and karate. I am from quiet places and laughter too. I am Killian, a little warrior, smart, and strong. I am uniquely me. **I am enough. You are you, and you are enough, too.**

A picture I drew. A little bird in a tree. We are like birds, all different, but the same.

I AM ME

I am me. My name is Kincso Kohutics. I was born in Budapest, Hungary. I grew up in Nyiregyhaza, with my mom, dad, and close relatives. While my dad worked at Lego, and my mom at the Mustar Haz, my grandma would look after me from my mom's side. Once I turned two, I went to preschool. There my mom would drop me off on her way to work and then pick me up on her bike. Mom would always be sure to have something from the bakery stowed away in her basket for a bike ride snack. We would go home later, and my dad would get home, and we would have dinner. Almost a year later, my dad got promoted to a new job at Lego, but this meant, at age three, we moved to North America. The trip was long; two buses, two planes, one car, and we finally arrived in Suffield, Connecticut. I continued preschool and after a while, we moved to East Longmeadow, Massachusetts. I started gymnastics, which I grew to love, and also took Taekwondo.

Five years later, we moved again to South Windsor, Connecticut, where I live now. I started third grade, and I loved it. My dad kept his job, my mom stayed at home, and I went to school. Now here I am in fifth grade. I still love gymnastics, but have switched gyms. **Next year, I'll be going to sixth grade at Timothy Edwards, and can't wait. I Am Me.**

This picture was taken in Rhode Island. We were at East Beach. The photo was taken in front of one of Taylor Swift's summer vacation mansions.

Kyleigh Levy

I AM KYLEIGH

I am Kyleigh

I go to Pleasant Valley Elementary School.

I am in second grade.

My favorite color is blue.

I like to play with my friends.

I was born on May 14, 2014.

I am a little sister.

I have three siblings.

My family is from Jamaica.

I love hanging out with my siblings.

I drew myself when I'm happy.

ALL ABOUT MYSELF

My name is Leila. I have four people in my family! Eden, my sister, and my mom Marnie, and my dad Mathew and myself. My favorite colors are black and teal. My favorite shapes are a star and a heart. I like to play games like Roblox and Outfoxed and Guess Who. When it's nice outside, I like to go to the pool. And when it's cold, I like to play in the snow. In the summer is my birthday, and I've celebrated my birthday in many different places like Puerto Rico, Florida, Rhode Island, and this year I'll be in Maine! We like to watch movies as a family. My favorite special treats are donuts, candy, and chocolate. My favorite foods are mac and cheese, tacos, and dumplings.

I like to ride roller coasters. I went to Hershey Park for spring break, and it was so much fun! I rode the Sooper Dooper Looper and the Comet. I also went to Disney World and Universal, and there were a lot of rides. I liked all the Mountain rides at Disney. At Universal, Hagrid's motorcycle ride was my favorite. I also love to do gymnastics!

I'm in first grade, and my teacher is Ms. Devlin. She is so fun! I have two best friends, their names are Braelyn and Taryn. I like school. My favorite things are math, writing, reading and specials.

I am me!

Leila Hauschild

This is how flexible I am!

ALL ABOUT A KID NAMED LIAM

Liam Palmiter

My name is Liam, and I am eight years old and in second grade. I was born on October 22, 2013. My birthday is very close to Halloween every year, which is special and fun. I live with my mom, who is a teacher; my dad, who helps design engines for planes; my four-year-old sister Colleen, and my dog Maggie. In my family, I am the only grandson on both sides. I was also lucky enough to spend several years getting to know my great-grandmother before she went to heaven. I like different types of animals, including otters, seals, cats, and dogs. I also enjoy trying new foods whenever I can. Some of my favorite foods are lobster, shrimp, and mussels. In my free time, I play video games, practice karate, go to art school, and spend time with friends and family. In school, I do well in math, science, and reading. My teachers would say I am smart and kind-hearted, but I can also be a little too full of energy at times. I like to make lots of friends and love to make them laugh. Other words to describe me would be strong-willed, protective, friendly, creative, and determined. **These are just some of the things about me that make me one of a kind.**

for my eighth birthday, my grandma and grandpa took me on a whale watch. I had never been on one, so it was super cool to see all the different types of whales.

AN ORDINARY FRIDAY

Have you ever been asked to write a story about yourself? Well, here goes! My name is Liam Staroverov. I am ten years old—my lucky number! I am more than halfway through fifth grade, and I am looking forward to sixth grade. Some of my favorite hobbies are soccer, playing video games, and amusement parks.

I am the oldest of three siblings. One of the things I love about my family is we all love to have fun with each other. Here's a glimpse of a typical night with my family through this poem.

AN ORDINARY FRIDAY

Mom comes back from the store,
With a fresh plate of sushi.
Me and sis know what to do,
Have some fun and maybe more.

We put a finger full of wasabi on our sushi.
Ask our parents to record,
I know what's gonna happen…
I know what's in store.

We eat the sushi at the same time,
Trying to keep it in.
Don't let it fly.
I tuck it in, just like a tie.

I can feel the spiciness in my mouth.
I look at sis,
I want to shout.

Sister gagging,
Spits food out.
**I couldn't keep it in;
I had to shout.**

Liam is posing as a model during a family vacation for dad, who is a photographer.

Lisette Perras

THE PERRAS'S GO TO PARIS

Hi, my name is Lisette Perras (that's right, pronounced like Paris in France even though it is not spelled the same way!). I am eight years old and in third grade. My nickname is "Lisette-y Spaghetti!" I have two dogs. One is named Cedric (an English Bulldog that sounds like a potbelly pig) and the other is named Astrid (a mixed breed with stubby legs). I have three fish, love the smell of bacon in the morning, and enjoy sneaking cookie dough from the bowl when my parents and I are baking together, especially chocolate chip. My favorite food is lobster with butter, especially on New Year's Eve when I get to stay up late and keep my parents awake to watch the ball drop on television. I love to be outside bike riding, playing with my dogs, and practicing soccer since I am on a travel team. Also, I hike quite a bit with my parents because they want me to love nature. I like to try new things that can sometimes be a little scary, such as diving off the swim block to make the swimming team. Both sides of my family are quite French, and my Grandmama speaks French fluently. My Papa, who is deaf, is practically a superhero to me, and has a service dog named Nadia (a Wheaten Terrier). Me and my parents like to travel to places such as Arizona, California, New York, Vermont, Florida, and London. Hopefully there will be many new places for my and me to travel to together. I also love visiting the UConn Dairy Bar with my mom to get ice cream (we love UConn, she says we "bleed blue"). I hope to become a veterinarian someday, because animals are full of love and I want to give them love back. Art is one of my favorite subjects, and so my dad and I watch online tutorials to challenge each other to make all different types of pictures. I really love learning at Pleasant Valley and think it's super cool we have a mascot named Popcorn the Panther. Finally, I have earrings and a necklace that are mini Eiffel Towers, and even a lamp shade that has pictures of the Eiffel Tower on it! **I hope to travel to Paris someday with my family and see the Eiffel Tower! Au revoir!**

THE BABY OF THE FAMILY

Bonjour! Spasibo! Just in case you didn't realize, I just greeted you in two different languages: French and Russian. Bonjour and Spasibo means hello in English.

One of the things that makes me unique is the fact that my parents are from two different countries. My mom is from Haiti and she speaks both Creole and French. My dad is from Latvia, and he speaks Russian.

My name is Lucas Nikolai Staroverov but my family calls me Luca. I am the youngest of three. I want to let you in on a little secret. Being the baby of the family is awesome. I get to do some cool things that other five year olds don't get to do, like riding scary rides at the amusement park because I have older siblings.

My favorite thing to do is play with my toy cars and build with Lego blocks. I love playing pretend with my toy cars. I sometimes involve one of my siblings or my mom or my dad to join my world of imagination, but I'm pretty content being able to have "me" time.

Although I have moments where I can play quietly on my own or with one of my siblings, I also have lots of energy. I like to play soccer, work out with my dad, ride my bike around the cul-de-sac, and keep up with my older brother and sister.

Being the youngest has helped me to have confidence, be brave, and be empathetic. **I am grateful to be part of my family.**

Lucas at Myrtle Beach during a family photoshoot. This photo sums up his personality.

Lucksiya Kannan

THE CRAZY CRAFTER LUCKY

Hi, my name is Lucksiya Kannan (Lucky). I am blessed with a loving little sister, Diya (four years old), a caring mom, and a cool dad.

I'm a ten-year-old girl who, apparently, is fond of unicorns and mythical animals. To name a few, dragons and phoenixes (I think dinosaurs are still alive). I adore reading (I recently read Greek Gods, written by Rick Riordan. My favorite character is Percy Jackson) and I love playing with my best friends.

Moving on, I LOVE crafting; it's my specialty. I am a CRAZY crafter and I like to use items from the recycling bin to make the crafts. Give me a few supplies and tape and I will whip together anything you want. Honestly, I stash things up on my shelves (I know it's messy, but I NEED it). Making arts and crafts with my best friends is always a BLAST!

I also speak, not one, but TWO languages. Those are Tamil and English. Just in case you want to say 'hello'

in Tamil, it's Vaanakkam (வணக்கம், in our Tamil letters). I want to have a job that has SOMETHING to do with animals, cause I love them! I guess you could call me an animal lover.

Water is my BFF! I love everything about swimming. I admit; I'm not the, what do you call it? A swimming EXPERT, but I am an expert learner.

For about eight years, I asked my mom to sing the same Tamil song at night (my dad got annoyed sometimes). My grandma even wrote a song FOR me! My mom makes up stories for my sister and me. It starts somewhere and ends up nowhere (asleep already zzz...).

And last but not least, I'm SUPER funny. **I love making my friends laugh.** Sometimes our laughter gets so loud, and our parents tell us we sound like loud bears!

I am a crazy crafter who stash up all interesting stuff in my cupboard (mostly from recycle bin) and makes beautiful crafts with my team (tools) scissors, hot glue gun, staples, art supplies, and tapes. Recently I built a big castle with Amazon carton boxes. Rainbow, a unicorn necklace I wear, and a photo frame in the picture are a few samples.

This is a picture of my family.

Madelyn Parizo

I AM BLESSED

Hi. My name is Madelyn Parizo. I am seven years old and in first grade.

I live with my Nana and Grandpa, who are also my mom and dad. They adopted me on National Adoption Day in November of 2019, but I have lived with them since I was a baby.

I have an older brother who is also my Uncle (due to my adoption). His name is Mitchell and he is twenty-six years old. He taught me how to play basketball, soccer, and baseball.

I have a cat named Pearl. We adopted her from the Connecticut Humane Society in 2021.

I take gymnastics and Hip Hop dance, which I enjoy a lot. I'm thinking about taking karate in the fall.

My nationality is French, Irish, and Japanese. My dad is half Japanese and my mom is French. My grandma in Florida is Irish.

I love school. I have lots of friends. My favorite thing to do is read. I have all the Junie B Jones books. She is my favorite character.

As a family, we love to go fishing for trout and go to the park and playground. In the summer, we go on vacation, and I love to go fishing at the shore!

I have lots of aunts and uncles and cousins. We get together on holidays.

I love the Christmas holiday the best! I have a special Christmas Eve box that I open on Christmas Eve. It's filled with all kinds of goodies and a new pair of pajamas to wear that night. This is a tradition that we have done since I was a baby.

I have a wonderful family. I am grateful for everyone in my life and how much they love and take care of me. **I am blessed.**

Madison

THE LIFE OF ME

My name is Madison and I'm in kindergarten. I have brown hair and am five years old. I live in South Windsor with my mom, dad, big sister, and our dog Mia. I have a big family with lots of cousins, aunts, uncles, and grandparents. We like to get together to celebrate holidays like Christmas, Hanukkah, Halloween, New Year, Easter, and Thanksgiving.

My family likes to eat together on the holidays. We eat chicken, turkey, and grilled cheese. We love to be outside when the weather is nice and eat out on our deck.

We take our dog for a walk and play in the backyard on our trampoline. I also like to ride my bike, play hopscotch, hula-hoop, ride horses, play ball, and go on the swings at the park.

My sister and I also go to Girl Scouts. In the fall, we like to go apple picking and get apple cider. My family enjoys baking cookies and making homemade pizza and smoothies. **Before bed, I like to snuggle with my parents and sister and read books.**

I love playing outside and in the pool under a rainbow.

KNOCK KNOCK: IT'S ME

I would like to share some interesting facts that makes me Maharvin. I think am a smart and humorous seven-year-old. I love to read and I am good at solving mathematical equations. I am one of the fast runners in my classroom and neighborhood. I like riding my seven-speed gear bike.

I love talking about space; it is educational and fun to learn about. I want to be an astronomer when I grow up!

I also want to be an author when I grow up. I am already one right now; I want to write novels and chapter books for children.

I love learning about animals—living and extinct. My great-grandfather, from my dad's side, is known as the greatest anthropologist in Asia. My great-great-grandfather, from my mom's side, was a freedom fighter who worked with Mr. Gandhi. He followed non-violence to free India from the British.

You know what are my favorite times? When I spend time with my dad answering trivia about geography, animals, spelling, and other things before bedtime. It makes me feel happy and relaxed. I love when my mom takes me to the park and when we play badminton. It is so much fun!

I also love to play sports. My favorites are tennis and soccer. I am really good at these two sports. I also play

Maharvin Sarkar

My Lego X-Wing Fighter

the piano. I don't really like playing piano, but my dad says I play it very well. I build a lot of Legos. I even built a Star Wars X-Wing Fighter!

I love telling jokes. My favorites are "Knock Knock" jokes (I am sure you saw the title) and have a collection of various jokes.

I have learned that everyone is unique just the way they are, and we must not feel sad if we are different. **I love myself and I am sure you do too!**

Malem Thokchom

I AM MALEM

My name is Malem Ngnanba Thokchom. I was born on 21st July 2016, which was one of the hottest days of the hottest month of the hottest year in 137 years in history. Everyone calls me Malem. Only my dad calls me Malemba. My mom sometimes calls me Thoiba, which means sweet boy.

I am lucky! I am the youngest of three siblings! My big sister is Sania and my big brother is Jason.

My parents are from Manipur, a tiny state in the northeast region of India. So, I am the first generation in my family's American history.

I love Halloween for costumes and candies. Spiderman is my favorite Superhero! I love Xmas for the tree and gifts. I enjoy when our family celebrates ethnic Manipur festivals. Some of my favorites are Yaoshang/Holi festival, Cheiraoba for New Year, and Chakouba, a grand feast and gifts, which I like the most. In the U.S., we celebrate these festivals together with some family friends.

I go to karate class at Clayton's Kenpo Karate. Last fall, I went to soccer club, which I enjoyed as I got ice cream after soccer lessons.

The best outing I enjoyed the most was rock climbing during the recent spring break with my sister's friends. I could climb all the way to the top!!!! I love playing at the beach, digging to create ponds and swimming in the ocean waves with my dad and sister.

I really like playing with Lego blocks and building things. The best is I have built a house with an attached garage.

I love yard work! Another thing I love that we do is deck camping with my dad and family and fireside dining on our deck!

Well, that's about it. I am me, Malem! More to come as I grow!

Pictures of my story! Things I do and I like!

I AM MANSI

On Mar 3, 2011, I was introduced to the world at Manchester Memorial Hospital. My mom says I was an easy baby but grew up to be a trouble-making toddler. Now I am eleven. My mom sometimes calls me Jingles and my dad sometimes calls me Jinglee. My favorite food is macaroni and cheese, especially from Olive Garden.

I am talented. I like to draw, craft, play piano and cello, write stories, and dance. I mostly write realistic fiction. I've been playing piano since I was five years old and cello since I was nine years old. My feet can't stop moving. I've been dancing since I was three. I started just doing ballet and added tap when I was five. Because of COVID, our 2020 Spring Showcase got canceled. We had already started practicing the dances. I was mad at COVID because everything just shut down. We didn't even have a 2021 Spring Showcase. At least this year's show is on. We finished all the parts to our ballet dance and just have a little bit left of our tap dance.

I want to be a baker and an author when I grow up. I've already written some stories, even when I was a toddler, although those made no sense to anybody else. I've baked cakes, cupcakes, and cookies with my mom. I am allergic to all tree nuts except for coconuts. That is why I will have a nut-free bakery. We only buy cakes and cupcakes from the Stop &

Shop bakery because most of what they have is nut-free. When I go to someone else's house and there is cake, we have to ask them if it has nuts in it.

My parents and my brother were born in India. We speak Tamil. I call my mom Amma and my dad Appa. I go to Tamil class, but I don't speak Tamil. I just know a lot of Tamil words. My parents want me to speak Tamil, but I am better at writing it. My mom thinks my Tamil handwriting is better than hers. It actually is.

Did I already say I am a bundle of energy? I can't stop bouncing around on the exercise ball or even jumping and doing gymnastics on the sofa. My parents have to yell at me to calm my body. **This is who I am. I am Mansi.**

This is me reading during distance learning. The in-person kids were also reading outside because it was warm.

Mathieu Lydecker

MY NAME IS MATHIEU

My name is Mathieu Lydecker and I am eight. I am in third grade. My teachers have all been nice. I like stuffed animals. I have over 100 stuffed animals, and my favorite one is my tiger. I have a lot of friends. I like to play with my brother, and I like to ski. I also like to play baseball, write, and to read. I like fiction books but not non-fiction. My favorite color is light blue, like the sky shade of light blue. I like dessert and roller coasters. I like to swim because it is relaxing and refreshing. It is really fun. I want to grow a tree on a diving board and climb it and jump into the pool, because I like to climb trees. I really want a treehouse. I like to tackle my friends and fool around. My favorite holidays are Christmas and Halloween, because I like candy and presents. I always get good presents and candy.

I like to tell jokes and I have a good sense of humor. I am good at video games. I am smart and good at math. I am silly and funny and I am part of the "Crazy Kids." I once walked under a bridge in freezing cold water in early spring with normal clothes on and it was up to my waist. That was when the "Crazy Kids" were formed.

I have a cool house with a big basement. I have a brother, a mom, and a dad. My brother is named Jackson and he is ten and in fifth grade. My mom is named Karen and my dad is named Daniel. My grandma speaks English and French and she is from Canada. I have two cats named Smokey (boy) and Mia (girl). I am getting a new cat for my birthday.

I have been to an adventure park a few times and went about 55 feet in the air. My Uncle Eric taught me how to ski by making me hold on to his pole and he skied down the mountain. Now I can ski really fast. **My uncle is silly and likes to play chase with my brother and me.**

This is a picture of my stuffed animal Tiggy.

I AM MAVERICK

Maverick Grisevich

I am Maverick. My friends call me Mav. I live in a small, white house in South Windsor, CT. I live with my mom and my dad. I am funny, caring, kind, smart, and a very fast runner. I love reading books, because I picture a movie in my mind when I'm reading. My favorite subjects are math and science. I want to code computers to make fun apps and games when I grow up.

I am just like any ordinary seven-and-a-half-year-old: I love to play video games, ride my bike, swim, hike, camp, climb trees and explore in the woods. I especially like to make tree forts. My grandpa is building a cool fort in the woods behind my house. The fort is made of tree limbs, tree bark, twigs, and vines. When we are in the woods, that is our base camp, where we pretend that we are exploring the unknown.

There is one super special thing about me that you should know. I am allergic to peanuts. I was one-year-old when I ate peanut butter. I started to get hives and had trouble breathing. I was too little to remember, but my parents told me I rode in an ambulance to the hospital. I go to the doctor every year to test and see if I am still allergic to peanuts. I have to be careful of what I eat, and I get to carry around an Epi-pen, which will help to save my life if I eat a peanut accidentally. **Lastly, I AM MAVERICK!!**

This is me, Maverick, at the Stonington lobster trap tree at Christmas 2021. It was so bright and colorful, I had a great time with my Mimi!

Michael Beaudoin

I AM MICHAEL SAVVAS BEAUDOIN

My name is Michael Savvas Beaudoin. I was born on May 7, 2014. I have a twin brother named Alex. My dad chose the name Michael because it is his middle name. My mom chose my middle name because that is her dad's name, my papou, which means grandpa in Greek.

I am in second grade and attend Pleasant Valley School. I have met so many friends there, and I love playing with them. I enjoy playing video games. I also have some great friends that live near my grandparent's house. I am lucky to be able to go and stay there
a lot and play with the kids in that neighborhood. We jump on trampolines, play basketball, race bikes and scooters, and have a lot of fun!

When I grow up, I want to be an entrepreneur, a Realtor, own many businesses, and may even be a lawyer like my dad. I want to be able to do it all!

My mom says I am very thoughtful and helpful. I love to help people. I help my dad, my uncle, and my papou with yardwork. I do chores around the house, like to make my bed and set the dinner table too.

I really love to learn new things. I am learning to speak Greek. I am also learning piano and listen to all types of music. I like classical music and Greek folk music, but I do love everyday American music, too!

When I can, I like to spend time with my family, especially my grandma (Yiayia) and grandpa (Papou). I love to stay with my godmother and uncle too. They are very special to me. We have big yummy breakfasts when I am there. **When I am there, they make me feel special and loved.**

This is me! I am seven years old and love to learn new things and play all day!

MY FAMILY FROM AROUND THE WORLD

Michael Salazar

My mom was born on the other side of the world in Ho Chi Minh, Vietnam. She came here with my brother before I was born a long time ago. My dad was born in Juarez, Mexico, 2000 miles away from here. My mom doesn't speak Spanish and my dad does not speak Vietnamese. My brother is lucky because he can speak Vietnamese, English, and a little Spanish. My grandma also lives with us. She can only speak Vietnamese, so it's very fun to communicate at home when everybody speaks different languages.

We have a lot of different food because we have a lot of different cultures. I like Vietnamese pho, Mexican enchiladas, and American hamburgers. To complete our family, we have two dogs named Scooby and Snowe. We also have three fish called Fishy. I love to swim, so I go to swim classes every week to get better at swimming. I am so lucky because I had the opportunity to swim with dolphins this spring break in Mexico.

This is my family and me, Michael Nguyen Salazar, 50 percent Mexican, 50 percent Vietnamese, and 100% American!

My family during Christmas. We took a picture together with all of us when we opened our presents.

Michaela Augustyn

MAGICAL ME

I am Michaela. I love unicorns. I love playing at the beach, building sand castles, and running into the water. I am a dancer, an ice skater, and a soccer player. I have a family that loves me. My dog, Finn, wags his tail and licks my face when he sees me. My cat, Cooper, snuggles with me every night. One of the most magical things about me though is that I am actually a ...

Unique

Nice

Interested in a lot of different things

Calm

Open

Respectful

Never give up

At my sixth birthday party, a real-life unicorn showed up, because I believe in unicorns! My belief in unicorns makes me special because I give them their magic.

I AM A MARSHALL

I am Michala Marshall but my family calls me Mickie.

I think that they call me Mickie, because I love Minnie and Mickey Mouse.

I am seven years old and the little sister to two big brothers. Can you guess who they are?

Well, let me tell you. My older brother's name is Justin and my younger brother's name is Jayce.

My mom and grandparents are from the beautiful island of Jamaica. My dad, brother's and I were all born in Connecticut, USA.

I love that I am of American and Jamaican heritage because it makes me feel super special!

I visited Jamaica with my parents, brothers, and grandma when I was three years old.

It was my grandma's sixtieth birthday. I was excited, and it was so much fun!

I went to the beach, tasted jerk chicken, listened to reggae music by Bob Marley, and even climbed Dunn's River Falls. I was only three years old, but I remembered it as if it was yesterday.

I am also an All-American Athlete.

My favorite sports are gymnastics, dance, track and field, and softball.

This year I went to an Indoor National Track and Field Meet and became All-American in all three of my events. I couldn't believe that I did! My parents, brothers, and grandparents were all super proud of me.

Michala Marshall

I love being an athlete, but, most importantly, I love being a kid, spending time with my family and having fun. Join me and learn all about my adventurous story!

I am energetic, kind, and caring, but most importantly, I enjoy helping others.

I want to become a doctor when I grow up but not just any type of doctor.

I want to become a Neurosurgeon, because I find the human brain to be very fascinating!

I know that with hard work, one day, my dream will come true to become a doctor.

I am Michala Marshall and I hope that you enjoyed my story.

Mona Madhan Raj

I, ME, MYSELF

Hi! My name is Mona. I was born on March 22, 2016, in India. My mommy tells me that I was the most beautiful baby she had seen. When I was three years old, I moved to the USA with my mommy and daddy. Saying bye to my grandparents was hard, but I also love my home in South Windsor, Connecticut. I have a little sister and her name is Nyra. She is four months old and was born in Manchester, Connecticut. I love her so much, I like to play with her. I also help mommy take care of her.

I love biking, crafts, drawing, and putting together jigsaw puzzles. I also love the beach and collecting seashells. My favorite colors are pink and purple. My favorite seasons are spring and summer. I love to do gardening with daddy.

I enjoy celebrating festivals with family and friends. My favorite Indian festivals are Diwali and Holi. Diwali is the festival of lights and it is also celebrating the victory of good over evil. The best part of Diwali is bursting fireworks. Holi is the festival of colors and love. It also represents the start of spring. Mommy makes

This is me enjoying fireworks during my favorite Indian festival Diwali.

Indian sweets during festival days. My favorite sweet is Kaju Katli (made out of cashew nuts and sugar).

Saturday nights are family nights. We order pizza and play UNO cards. We also sing and dance together. My mommy always tells me to do what I love, no matter what others think. **When I grow up, I want to become a singer and a doctor and help my community.**

NEW BEGINNINGS

My name is Myles. My parents are both from Jamaica, but I was born in Connecticut. I came to Pleasant Valley on September 1, 2021. Since I've come to Pleasant Valley, I have improved as a student. It is still hard for me to sit in school and do certain things but my amazing teachers Mrs. Augustyn, Ms. Peck, Dr. Farris, Miss Fazzino, and Mrs. Caouette help me grow and learn in school even when things are hard. Sometimes I just need a quiet place without people to get work done. Dr. Farris and Mrs. Caouette help me with that.

When I'm not in school I draw and play games or read a book. I don't really have a favorite thing to draw. I like to draw whatever comes into my mind. For instance, if I was watching TV a person or thing might randomly appear in my mind and I would want to draw it. Sometimes I wait until the next day to draw something at school because I like my art supplies that are at school. I don't know why my mind jumps around; it's just random.

Sometimes, I think about what I'd like to do when I grow up. One idea is to be a principal so I can tell people what to do. I would schedule events that little kids would enjoy. For instance, I'd have a costume contest and the person with the best costume would get a bag of candy with parents' permission. **I'd also make ice cream free to everyone every day.**

This is me at the beginning of fourth grade when I started at Pleasant Valley.

Noah Girouard

I LOVE MY FAMILY AND THE PLACES WE GO

My name is Noah Girouard and I'm eight years old. I have brown hair and big brown eyes. I am Acadian; my great-great-grandparents were French Canadians that settled in northern Maine. My mom's parents still live in northern Maine and my uncle and many of my cousins live there too. We visit them every summer and sometimes go for Christmas. Our trip to Maine, in July, is one of our family traditions. We swim in the lake, play with cousins, go fishing with my Memere, and we play outside a lot. I love throwing rocks into the lake with my little sister, Hannah. My older brother Jameson and I go tubing with our cousins behind my Pepere's Jet Ski. It is super fun. I could ride on the tube all day. My dad's parents live in CT and we see them often. They have a boat and when we visit them on their boat, we get to swim in the river and play on the beach. I love the sand and I want to be a Paleontologist one day. I also love to play video games, and I learn technology super fast. I love pizza and hot dogs and cucumbers and peaches and vanilla-frosted donuts with sprinkles.

I love my family because we do things together. When we eat at the table, we ask trivia questions and everyone gets a turn to answer. We also like telling riddles and jokes at the dinner table. We play cards, like Go Fish and UNO. And we play board games.

This is my brother and me on the tube, being pulled by my Uncle Todd on the Jet Ski. The lake is the best place to go tubing.

My current favorite is Dino Challenge, a board game that has questions you have to answer about dinosaurs. **I love my family very much.**

I'M NOT JUST A BROTHER

My name is Oscar. My brother Owen and I are identical twins, and I am the younger one, but only by ONE minute. Even though I'm the younger one, I am probably stronger, and I lost the first tooth. I am also three years older than my little brother, Landon. I like to go camping with my family and with my Grandma and Poppy. Once I found a hammer at the campground and I brought it home! I sure do love to collect all sorts of tools! One day I hope to be a carpenter so I can build and fix anything I want. I'm saving my money to buy a particular nail gun.

I am so good at soccer that I made the travel team with my brother, Owen. I'm pretty good at whistling and I'm very good at riding my bike. My favorite subject in school is math. I'm very good at adding and subtracting, but I'm still learning how to multiply and to divide. I also like to play games on my tablet and sometimes I have to help my brothers move to the higher levels!

Some of my favorite foods are cheese doodles, smoothies, puffed pancakes, and General Tso's chicken. My mom has made me 2080 smoothies (and counting) since I was born! Can you believe it!? **My favorite color is orange. What is your favorite color?**

Me, Landon, and Owen on our porch on a rainy day. I'm the one whistling and wearing orange shorts with my soccer jersey.

THE STORY ABOUT ME: OWEN SOARES

Me, holding a delicious six-pound candy corn bag with silly Halloween glasses on just to make my Great Aunt laugh.

My name is Owen. I have an identical twin brother named Oscar that I don't always like having, but I always love him. I am probably stronger than Oscar. I also have a younger brother named Landon and he's only four years old. I am an excellent big brother to them both … when I want to be!

I am smart, artistic, and I love building Lego structures and drawing because I can create almost anything out of them. I also love to build the Nintendo Labo I got for Christmas because I get to follow the directions and I am challenged to get to the finished product. It is hard work, but, in the end, I get to play with it!

I like to play soccer because my dad is going to be my coach. I also like to help my dad fix our old tractor in our barn. I like puffed pancakes because my mom makes it and I love my mom and I love that she makes it for our family!

I am Owen. I am a jokester. **I only like candy corn when they come in a six-pound bag!!!**

MY BIG FAMILY

Hello! My name is Prajakta, and today I am going to share the uniqueness of my family.

Meet my family, which includes my mom, dad, and my little brother Arshith. I love my family and they are my strength. I have a very, very big family.

In my mom's family, my grandma, whose name is Archana, has four brothers and sisters. Sha also has eight cousin brothers and sisters. My mom has thirty cousins, brothers, and sisters. Now all of them are married and they have kids. So I have fifty cousins in my family. Isn't this a big number?

One funny thing I want to share with everyone:
My mom's uncle, who is staying in San Diego;
even though he is young, I used to call him Grandpa.
He has a twelve-year-old son.
I call him my Ishaan (uncle)! Ha ha ha!

But that is the beauty of our relationship. All my relatives and cousins used to attend functions, such as a marriage party or Thread ceremony in the family. I love to meet them, though I can't remember their names. It's really great to have such a big and loving family.

In my dad's family, my grandpa has eighteen cousin-brothers and six cousin-sisters, and they are my dad's uncles and aunties. He has around fifty cousins in total.

Prajakta Dash Sahu

My great-grandma's name is Sajni, and she is 101 years old. She loves me very much. She is very sweet and she is the oldest person in our family. That's all. **I love my FAMILY!**

My big family of my Mom and Dad.

Pranshie Shah

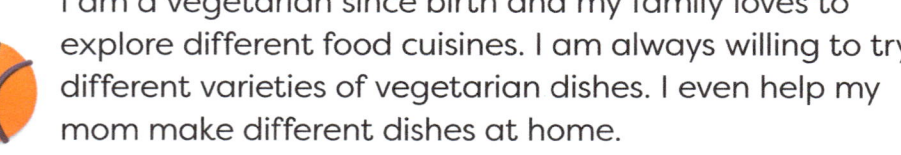

I AM....

I Am ... Pranshie. I am a fifth-grader in my AWESOME school. I love school so much that I get really upset when it is canceled sometimes because I don't get to meet my friends and learn something new. My school is like a second home to me.

My best personality traits are being kind, helpful, caring, loving, and funny. I am outspoken and sociable and make friends very easily. I am a little reluctant to change and since I set many high standards for myself, sometimes when I don't meet my own expectations, I feel frustrated and possibly angry. But my mom teaches me to make my rigid personality into my strength and always look at every situation positively and learn from them.

My parents are from India, and, the language I speak at home is called Gujarati, which comes from a state in India called Gujarat. I love learning languages and am taking lessons for Hindi and Japanese. I am also learning Spanish, Greek, and Latin on an online platform.

I am a vegetarian since birth and my family loves to explore different food cuisines. I am always willing to try different varieties of vegetarian dishes. I even help my mom make different dishes at home.

For activities, I LOVE to read, write, draw, and play basketball. My favorite thing to draw is people. My favorite book is *As Old As Time* by Liz Braswell. I have two bookshelves filled with books that I have read multiple times. I am writing many books and that again comes from my love for books. Basketball is my favorite sport and defense is my strength. Dance and swimming are after that. I learn an Indian form of dance called Bharatnatyam, which is one of the oldest and most popular forms of classical dance that originated in South India.

My curiosity to learn and my excitement to experience different and new things makes me ... **Uniquely ME!!!!!!!!!**

"Drawing at its best is not what your eyes see but what our mind understands" – Millard Sheets.

Life is fun and easy – Eat, Sleep, Play Basketball, Repeat. I love my colorful clothes and all the accessories I get to wear for my dance performances.

A GIRL WITH A LOT OF DREAMS

Prarthana Paulraj

About eight years ago, on October 20, 2013, I was born in the city of Tirunelveli, which is close to the Southern tip of India, which was my Mom's place. My parents named me "Prarthana" which means "Prayer." When I was about three months old, I moved to Chennai, India, which was my Dad's place. Then when I was one-and-a-half, I moved to the USA.

I have an older brother named Pranav, who I call Anna. In Tamil, Anna means Big Brother.

In India, people speak a lot of different languages. We speak Tamil in our home; it is our native language. So, here in the USA, I started taking a class to learn Tamil. I can understand and read Tamil, but I cannot speak or write it that well. I would also like to learn Japanese. I like to draw and play board games. When I grow up, I want to be a lot of things like an FBI agent, an actor, or a movie director.

I love Indian savory foods because they are very interesting. My favorite Indian food is pidi kozhukattai. It is like a dumpling but not stuffed. It can be made either spicy or sweet but my favorite is spicy. It is made out of rice flour and steam cooked. Other foods I like are poori and appam.

I have a lot of hobbies like arts and crafts.

Myself in Cliffwalk, RI with my favorite flower – Daffodils.

I like to do inspirational drawings, which is taking inspiration from things. Another one is singing, but I don't like singing in front of people.

I wish everyone in this world would be nice to each other and everyone should have a family and a home.

Prisha Rajesh

I AM PRISHA, PRISHA RAJESH!!!

Prisha Rajesh and her little sister, Tanvi Rajesh, posing for fall colors.

I am Prisha Rajesh. Right now, I am nine years old. My parents are both from India, but I was born in Chicago on July 30, 2012. I love school and all my teachers! I enjoy reading fantasy books, especially the series "Princess Pulverizer." I used to go to Taekwondo, chess, swimming, tennis, and Kumon. I still go to RSM (Russian School of Math) and Tamil classes. I speak English, a little bit of Tamil, and a little bit of Spanish. I understand Telugu and Tamil. I love my family, friends, Tanvi (my sister), and LOL Dolls.

My name means "Gift of God," but the letters in my name also stand for my characteristics.

Persevering because when I am doing my RSM math homework and I get stuck, I try my best before asking my mom or dad.

Respectful because I try my best to listen to teachers. When the teacher is talking, I listen and then I ask questions.

Intelligent because I try to challenge my brain. Like when there was a challenge in my math packet and it was optional, I just wanted to do it.

Silly because I want my friends to smile all the time. When all my friends are worried, I make them laugh and smile. I want them to be happy forever.

Humorous because I love to laugh and smile.

Amazed because I observe and am amazed by science. For example, I was amazed at Mystic Aquarium when I touched different textures on the sea animals and they were all so different.

I love candy and my sister (but I love my sister more than candy). My sister, Tanvi, likes movies with no fighting and no death. If she watches a movie with fighting, she will cover her ears, close her eyes, and sing loudly ¨LA LA LA.¨ My favorite thing to watch on TV is Spongebob.

One of the best things about me, though, is I try to be a good friend and kind to others!

My florida trip. I went with my family to Sea World and saw cute dolphins. I stood with muppets from Sesame Street.

Raina Senthilkumar

I AM ME

I am Raina, and I like dogs and love penguins. In my family, I have a big brother named Rishi and he is eleven years old. I have a mom named Preethi. I have a dad named Senthil. I have the nickname, "Puppy," because I like dogs. I see myself and my family in a positive way because we always like to keep things clean and tidy (especially my dad) and be happy for each other. The beauty in my family is that we always are together (except for in school) to protect each other. My family is unique because we are Indian and speak a different language called Tamil. My family likes to go to pet stores and look at very cute animals and we like to play a game on all nights called Monopoly. The top three words to describe my family are beautiful, friendly, and wonderful. Something my family and I will accomplish is BUYING a new house with a new dog named Lucky in it. Some traditions we have are girls wear a dot on their forehead, which is called a bindi and it represents protecting the girls.

We make a certain type of dish called idly. It's a type of Indian food that is pretty soft and is served with any type of curry called dal sambar. And that is the end of my I am me project. **I hope you liked it!**

Reyansh Bardhan

I AM REYANSH

Hello! I'm Reyansh Bardhan, a fourth-grader at Pleasant Valley School. I am excited to share about 'who I am.' To start with, let me share about my family.

We are a family of four: mom, dad, my sister (Shanaya), and myself. My parents are originally from Kolkata (city of joy), India. My grandparents and other relatives live in India and visit us sometimes. As a family, we have lots of fun and we love to travel to new places.

Knowing myself for around ten years, some of my traits are artistic, humorous, and friendly. One thing I am passionate about is guitar. I take guitar lessons and have learned around seventeen songs to date. Besides guitar, karate lessons excite me a lot. Along with regular karate lessons, I take karate leadership classes which means I help other kids during their classes. Another secret about me is that

Me and my sister on a family vacation.

I tried writing poems. Fortunately, I won poem contests in kindergarten and in first grade.

Among several traditional activities, my parents make foods that are special to our family. For example, my mom's "luchi" (a Bengali flatbread) or my dad's mutton biryani (an Indian dish with rice and goat meat) are very "yummy." We celebrate all U.S. holidays as well as Indian holidays such as Durga Puja and Diwali.

When I grow up I want to be an author. I love to read big chapter books and have finished the Harry Potter series. Some of the other books that I like are the Percy Jackson series, the Magic Treehouse, and the Heroes of Olympus. My friends and family say that I am funny and I enjoy jokes. I like lots of different foods such as pasta, chicken wings, and pizza.

So, that is pretty much about myself. **I know I am special in my own way. I am Reyansh (or you can call me Rey Rey).**

I LOVE MY FAMILY

Ridhi Bevara

I am Ridhi. I love doing art, wearing fancy dresses, and baking cakes. I also like making pizza and jelly with my family. I love to watch Disney movies with my family. I also love to grow plants.

I dislike when people yell at me or when they don't want to play with me.

I love my Dad because he makes my favorite cheese pizza, takes us camping, and makes us chicken curry. He also plays with us in the park.

I love my Mom because she keeps the house tidy, cooks yummy food, teaches me to sing, and dances with me.

I have a little brother who shares toys with me and makes me laugh by being silly.

One thing all of us in my family love to do is to grow our own veggies and flowers in the summer. We grow plants organically without harmful chemicals so that we can eat healthy food.

On our land, we grow vegetables like cucumbers, carrots, lady fingers, eggplants, tomatoes, and bell peppers, and flowers like sunflowers and marigolds. **I love helping Mom and Dad in planting, watering, and harvesting the plants every day.**

I have created art around my name.

Ram Utsav Desai

This is a picture taken by my mom on the morning of my sixth birthday, before I headed out for Pleasant Valley School.

I AM . . .

I AM ...

I am Ram Utsav Desai.

I am six years old.

I am in the first grade.

I am intelligent and love to learn new things.

I am a bird enthusiast and nature lover.

I am an amazing artist who can draw many different things.

I am a bird watcher.

I am a cook and make delicious lemonade.

I am a non-fiction book reader.

I am a writer and enjoy creating informational books.

I am a food eater. I enjoy eating North Indian dishes, especially Paneer Makhani with buttery garlic naan.

I am unique because I have a bubbly personality.

I am a beach lover. I enjoy being under the sun and in the big ocean.

I am sweet and love to hug and cuddle with my mom and dad.

I am kind-hearted and my teachers tell me I have a heart of gold.

I am grateful for this nice life.

I am Ram Utsav Desai.

ME, FAMILY, AND OUR CUSTOM

Rishik Krishna

"Rishik!" "Rishik!" slowly my dad called me and woke me up around 4:45 a.m. on April 15. I remembered that it's our cultural festival "Vishu" today, which is celebrated in the Indian state of Kerala. On the day of Vishu, it is a custom to wake up very early in the morning, with closed eyes, and then slowly open the eyes to see the glorious view of God first thing in the morning, along with oil lamps, vegetables, fruits, grains, money etc. It is called "Vishukkani," signifying the beginning of a new year.

You know what rituals I like the most on that day? Getting money from my parents, spending time with family members and friends, and having delicious food with them. Back in India, children burst firecrackers early in the morning or the prior night. So, this year, as always, my parents and I woke up early in the morning and did the main ritual and prayed for a new peaceful and prosperous year ahead. The good part of technology is that we can see and talk to our family members, no matter how far they are. We have an extended family and we had a video chat with them and shared our photos with each other and my mom also made a lot of vegetarian dishes with a little help from my side and more help from my dad.

I was waiting for my friends and their family to join us for the feast called as "Sadhya," and finally here they are! We had the feast together on a banana leaf as a part of the custom and after that, we all had a nice time until we were all tired and sleepy. **Before I went to sleep, I told my mom the food was so delicious, as always, with a lot of hugs and kisses!**

Me celebrating "Vishu," our traditional Malayali New Year.

Rosie Guerino

ALL ABOUT ROSIE

My name is Rosie. My favorite colors are red and pink. I really like my two sisters and one brother. I like school. I am in kindergarten. We have forty-five days left of school. This summer I am going to a family wedding. We will get to stay at a hotel with a pool. I am looking forward to swimming lessons. We swim in the ocean. **I am so excited for first grade.**

Ready for swimming lessons in my pink bathing suit and holding my baby sister.

ME AND MY FAMILY

Saipragna Reddy Madina

I am Saipragna Reddy Madina. My family and friends call me Sai. I am a fourth-grader at Pleasant Valley School, Connecticut. Do you know the meaning of Pragna in my name? It means wisdom. That's why I like to build my knowledge and have good judgment; that is being wise. I am a cute Texan girl born on December 20, 2012, at 10:49 a.m. We moved to Connecticut in 2015 because my parents had a lot of opportunities in this place and most importantly, we wanted to stay together. I love reading, watching documentaries and exploring new things. My favorite color is pink and my favorite food is pizza. My hobbies are dancing, playing the piano, singing, and making art. My favorite sports are swimming and badminton. I always feel proud to be a Pleasant Valley student.

My parents migrated from India and settled here. I always listen to my parents because they are my best friends and mentors. I have a big family in India, with many relatives and cousins. We follow our culture, festivals, and traditions. I am attending Prajna classes to know about our ancient culture and traditions. My favorite festival is Diwali, which we call the festival of lights, it symbolizes the victory of good over bad. We love to spend time together and share things. My parents always say things won't come readily; to achieve something I need to focus and constantly work hard. My parents always ask me to set smaller goals and complete them in time with happiness. I love my family; my family is one of my strengths.

I love reading all genres of books and watching discovery documentaries which help me to improve my knowledge. When I am nervous, I like to relax and watch programs that make me happy. Recreational activities help me to boost my energy levels. I know what I want to be in my life. I want to become a doctor and serve people. At the same time, I want to explore novel things. I am very happy to write this little story about my family and me. **I would like to thank my teachers and my friends for supporting and helping me.**

This is me trying to explore myself in the reflection.

Samantha Hubbard

Me and Lucas!

I AM SAMANTHA HUBBARD

I have a big family. We value spending time together with our pets. I love animals.

My favorite animal is a sea turtle. We have seven pets. We have three dogs, three cats, and a turtle. My family loves having pets. Lucas, our vizsla is my favorite pet. He's almost three years old. I love snuggling with Lucas. It's my favorite thing to do.

We take our pets on vacation and do lots of hikes with them. **Having and loving pets is awesome.**

I AM SAMANVI

It all started on June 21, 2016. I came into this world on this very day. As you all know, it's the first day of summer. My mom says when she saw me for the first time, she thought I was the cutest thing on earth. That's why she gave me the name "Samanvi." That means best of all. As my name says, I try to be the best in everything. I am the youngest and cutest girl in my family. I am a very kind, caring, and loving girl. I make friends very easily. Do you know? I have two best friends whom I have known almost from birth. Now they are in third grade, and they are my best buddies. If I don't see them or hear from them, I miss them a lot. They say you must make friends your age, but age was never a problem for us to become BFFs. My elder sister, who is in middle school, is a beautiful singer. Whenever I hear her singing, I want to be a singer when I grow up. I'm a good dancer too, you know. I like people, so I like to be surrounded by people. I love laughing and I love to make others laugh. **So, I always wish to have fun with my family and friends.**

Hello, It's me.

Samara Kennedy

Samara in front of her new home in Connecticut.

SIMPLY SAMARA....

I am Samara. My family calls me Sam-Sam or Sammy. I was born in Miami, Florida and at just two months old, I moved to Kingston, Jamaica with my family. I lived and went to school in Jamaica for five years. I loved going to the beach, but I do not like the crabs. Our family has a strong Jamaican accent, especially my grandpa in Jamaica. He is very, very funny! I have a large family with many grandparents, cousins, uncles, and aunts. I love eating mangoes! During COVID, we moved to South Windsor, Connecticut. I was very sad that we had to leave our old house and some of my family members. I miss the park in front of our house and being able to walk to my Uncle Kammy and Aunty Nicky's house and catch the butterflies. I swam with dolphins!

I now live with my mom, sister (Sekai), and two cats (Nathan and Holly). We visit Jamaica on our birthdays, weekends, and Christmas to see our family. Love, care, and respect are most important to my family. I am the loudest in my family and love to giggle. My family understands and loves me; they are funny and loving. I love helping my mommy cook in the kitchen and take care of the cats. I love her cheese omelets. **I am the funniest person in my family.**

WHAT MAKES ME, 'ME'

Hi, my name is Sanah. I was born in September of 2011. My parents are both from different parts of India, and they speak totally different languages. They both met here in America. I have a sister (who can be VERY annoying at most times), a mom, a dad (who probably feels a minority since he's the only boy) and my kitten, Libby. My family and I love to be outdoors. We go on hikes, and we spend a lot of time in our pool during the summer. My family has taught me to be hardworking, always be my best self, and to be punctual.

I love to swim. I'm on the swim team, and I swim for an hour every day. I also kinda like to do math. My parents call me a radio station; they say that if they give me a song, I can sing it, which I guess is true. I also like to read many different genres of books. I like graphic novels, mysteries, and Greek mythologies. My favorite place in school is the principal's office ;). I really like to eat cottage cheese and Burgers. Oh! And pizza, don't forget the pizza. I'm making my own mouth drool now. I love being/hanging out with my friends, and I even convinced my parents that we shouldn't move just so that I could stay with my friends. I play the viola, which is like a violin, but bigger and has lower notes. I also like to cook. I even have my own recipe on how to make potato French fries in the air fryer.

This is an exact quote from me, "One bug, and I'm outta the house." I HATE bugs. They're so tiny and disgusting, though I LOVE worms.

I am a very Special and Unique person, and I want to keep it that way. Oh, and as you probably can see, I talk a lot."

Almost every night, at like 10 p.m., I read for about twenty minutes. I remember this night, I had just come back from shopping with my family and I was EXHAUSTED 😭.

Sarah Gupta

I AM SARAH

My name is Sarah . I came into the world on June 12, 2015. I was born in Hartford, Connecticut U.S.A. There are three more people in my family: my mom, dad, and my cute little sister.

My mom's name is Monika Gupta. She is very helpful. She makes different hairstyles for me and she plays with me. She teaches me how to do all my work on my own. My dad's name is Rakesh Kumar. He does very hard work and helps me to learn math. My younger sister's name is Myra Gupta; she is very cute.

My sister is five years younger than me. She loves to play with me. I love her very much.

I love to do crafts, paintings, and drawings. I love going outside to pick some flowers. I love to go shopping with my family and buy LOL Dolls. My favorite color is purple. I love purple dresses. I don't like being alone. My favorite animals are squirrels, birds, and hamsters.

I'd love to spend more time with my family. **I LOVE MY FAMILY** 😘❤️

My family

UGADI THE TELUGU NEW YEAR

Sanvika Putchkayala

Ugadi: The Telugu New Year

The wind brushed through the trees and the flowers began to bloom. It was spring and it was Ugadi, too. The Hindu moms and dads began preparing for the pooja.

Mila, a young five-year-old, was sleeping while her parents were preparing for the pooja like everybody else in their small town. Mila's brother was trying to wake her up as her mother asked him to. Then she felt someone pulling the blanket off of her. It was cold and she was sleepy. She chased him down the stairs and to the kitchen but was stopped by her mom. "Stop right there Mila. If you want to get any farther, you have to take off your sandals!" Mila saw her brother sticking his tongue out at her, but she was too curious to stick it out right back. "Why do I have to take off my sandals to go into the kitchen?" She asked. "Your dad and I have been preparing for pooja all morning and if you go into the kitchen with your sandals, the gods will punish you because your sandals are dirty, and you are not supposed to go near the pooja mandir when you're dirty," Mila's mother said.

"Why are you preparing for pooja so early in the morning?" "Oh, it's Ugadi!" her mother replied. "What is Ugadi? What's the story of Ugadi?!" Mila pondered, then asked. "Ugadi means the Telugu new year in Sanskrit; it is also the beginning of spring! The story of Ugadi is that Lord Brahma started a creation with the Vedas, but then a demon stole the Vedas. So Lord Vishnu turned into an avatar and got the Vedas back to Brahma that day is now known as Ugadi!" her mother smartly noted. "WOW, that is amazing. I'm gonna go take off my sandals now!" Mila exclaimed.

She ran up the stairs as fast as she could, but on the way, she almost tripped over her dad. He was putting some type of leaves on the door! She was curious but said nothing. She took off her sandals when she was up in her room, then she ran back down and met up with her Dad at the door. This time she really wanted to know what he was doing so she said, "What are you doing, Dad?" "Oh, this? I'm putting up mango leaves." He happily said. "Why are you putting up mango leaves?" Mila asked, more curiously. Her dad started talking. "The leaves? Oh, they are used to keep the demons away, and also it is to keep bad luck out of our house."

"Have you ever heard the story of Lord Brahma? Well, basically…" she cut him off. "I heard it, Dad. I heard it when Mama told it to me." "Oh, ok, that's nice. Anyway, you look pretty dirty, you should take a bath." He said, changing the subject. "Ok, but do I have to?" she said, "Yes, of course, you have to, and you have to do it ahead of bath/shower," he said. "Awww." She protested. "I'll be there in five minutes!" her Mom said, from the kitchen. "Ok." She sighed.

After having oil applied by her mom, she showered with soap and water. Then, she dressed up traditionally, went downstairs, and did the pooja with her parents and brother. At breakfast, she asked why she had to do an oil bath. They said that Lord Laxmi resides in oil every day and Lord Ganga resides in water so if you do an oil bath you will be blessed by both goddesses. "That's nice," said Mila in awe.

Then the family all started to eat. She saw lemon rice, mango rice, tamarind rice, sweet pongal, curd, payasam, and something Mila didn't know. At least it smelled tasty! She stared at it so hard trying to figure out what it was that she didn't notice her father turn his head in her way, and then she heard him say, "That is Ugadi Pachadi." "Huh," she said finally. "That is Ugadi Pachadi," he said again. Without taking her eyes off the Ugadi Pachadi, she asked, "What is Ugadi Pachadi, Dad?" "Oh it's a type of pickle," he said simply. "It's not that simple, actually," her mom said, "It's the main festive food drink of Ugadi containing six ingredients, having the six flavors, representing the six emotions of life.

Sanvika Putchkayala, the author of this story

In the Ugadi Pachadi, there are:

   Tamarind – sour taste – unpleasantness

   Jaggery – sweet taste – joy or happiness

   Unripe mango – tangy – surprise

   Neem flowers – bitter – sadness

   Black pepper – spicy – anger

   Salt – salty – fear

"It is the first dish one has during the Ugadi festival after offering it to the deities. Apart from the health benefits of this festive drink, Ugadi Pachadi also signifies that one has to accept life with all its facets."

"Wow, now I know so much about Ugadi," Mila happily said, "Remember Ugadi is celebrated in many parts of the world, mostly in India!!!"

ALL ABOUT SARAYU

My name is Sarayu.

I was born on April 10, 2012, to two Indian parents at 1:30 a.m. in Hartford, Connecticut. I have a very funny little brother and I named him Taran, but he sometimes gets into a lot of trouble.

I live with my Mom, Dad, and my little brother. Some of my favorite things are art, coding, playing piano, playing violin, dancing, singing and playing with my brother, and having sleepovers with friends.

On Friday's, my family and I do Movie Night. Some of my favorite food are noodles, veg biryani, pizza, popcorn, and Happy Meals. My favorite Festivals are Diwali, Holi, and Christmas. I love to do fireworks on Diwali. We do so many fireworks. I love Holi so much because we throw Colors on other people. We get gifts on Christmas.

My favorite vacation places are Great Wolf Lodge and India.

family picture on my birthday, a picture on Holi with friends, and a Diwali fireworks picture.

Sarrinah Haque

I drew myself on the cover page.

I AM ME

My Name is Sarrinah Haque.
I am seven years old. My parents call me Lamiya at home. I have a younger brother. I love him so much. My mommy and daddy love me so much. I have a happy family. My dad always takes us on vacation to different places and gives us different activities. My favorite activities is playing in the park. I have a best friend. Her name is Arisha. We always play together.

My favorite food is chicken biryani. My mom is a good cook. She always cooks my favorite foods. My mom's food is very tasty and yummy. In my free time, I like to read books and draw pictures. Also, I like to watch TV and play with my brother.
I like to go to the beach. I enjoy nature viewing. I love my family. I always want to stay happy with my family. **God bless our family.**

I AM SARTHAK

On Thursday, May 14 2015, at 1:57 a.m., I came into this world. My name is Sarthak Singh. My family and friend call me Meethu. I was born in a hospital in Manchester, Connecticut. My parents and elder brother, Vaibhav (we call him Chiku), were born in India. My parents felt I completed the family, hence named me Sarthak. My brother is the best friend I could ever have. I love to play with him. We fight sometimes over small things and I get angry, but then he cooperates to make me happy. I love to share everything with him and make sure on my birthday we buy gifts he also likes. Without him being around, I can't imagine how boring a day could be. My brother says I am the most caring and loving brother he could ever have.

During winter, I love to play soccer and basketball in my basement with my brother and my dad. I love having fun fighting with dad when my brother and I fight together with dad to defeat him. In summer, I love going out on beaches and water parks. I get scared with dangerous slides, but my brother encourages me and makes me complete these slides with him. It is so fun just to be with him.

I love going to India and being around my cousins. I have four cousin-brothers, Lavi, Avi, Ravi, and Golu, and three cousin-sisters, Muskan, Riddhi,

I am six-year-old Sarthak. I love being with my brother Vaibhav and having fun together. I want to be a policeman when I grow up.

and Kuhu. We celebrate Holi and I love to color everyone's face with pichkari (color pump). We also celebrate Diwali and light our home with candle lights. I learned Hindi from Chiku and can talk fluently.

I want to be a policeman when I grow up, because I want to arrest criminals and help innocent people. I have a policeman uniform at home which I wear all the time until my mom takes it away to wash. I love gun toys and firing guns at a target. I can keep playing policeman the whole day with my brother around.

I go to Pleasant Valley School in the first grade. **I love my school, my class teacher Mrs Cyr, and my school friends.**

Sasha Staroverov

This picture was taken in front of our home by dad.

Music is something that brings my family together. **If you were to stop by our house on a Saturday morning, you will find us singing and dancing to all types of music while cleaning.**

MUSIC CONNECTS

My name is Sasha Grace Staroverov. The name Sasha is a pet name for Alexandra in Russian. A little more about me; I am eight years old, and I am in third grade. One of the best things about being a third-grader is making new friends and learning new things. I also love my teacher Ms. Dehaas who is funny and kind.

I live with my mom, my dad, my two brothers, and our guinea pig, Phil, and I love him. I am the middle child, and I am the only girl out of three siblings.

One of the things that makes me unique is that I am half Haitian and half Russian. I love being part of two different cultures because I get to listen to different types of music and eat all types of food. My favorite food is mashed potatoes.

Music is a big part of my family. My mom loves to sing and dance. I especially love when my parents host karaoke nights with family and friends because I get to sing with the grownups. I also sing in a children's choir at my church. It was lots of fun once I got over my stage freight.

This past Christmas, I had asked for an Alexa music player, because I wanted to listen to my own songs. It's been great not having to share with my brother. Now, I get to listen to the Encanto soundtrack as much as I want.

I'm Sashvanth. In Safari Park I'm feeding the bird.

I do not allow anyone to touch my racks because I'm scared of messing up my racks.

I'm new to the USA. I'm studying in grade two and still learning English. **I'm waiting to explore more new things.**

Sashvanth Balamurugan

SASHVANTH'S STORY

My Name is Sashvanth Balamurugan.

We have four people in our family.

My dad, my mom, and my little sister.

I like playing with my toy cars.

I love to play ball with my dad.

My family is too kind and too nice.

My dad is too patient and kind to me.

My mom cooks my favorite dishes.

My sister is a naughty girl. She plays with me and sometimes we fight with each other.

I watch TV and play video games.

I will do some crafts and drawings.

I have separate racks in my cupboard for me. I keep my books, my toys, and my belongings over there.

Savannah Goldstein

I AM ME

Who Is Savannah?

I am Savannah. I am nine years old and in fourth grade. I will be ten on October 5th. I live with both of my parents, Adam and Sarah, as well as my older siblings, Daytona who is fourteen and Austin who is twenty-one. I love my family with my whole heart, and I wouldn't change them for anyone else!

I can be sassy at times, but I am also polite, caring, spunky, unassuming, and kind. I like to keep busy with K-POP dance at my dance school. Dancing is a good workout that makes my body stronger and keeps me active, but I am most excited to have a recital to perform in front of an audience.

I think often about what I want to be when I grow up. I sometimes think about being an astronaut, but I know astronauts very rarely get to see their families and I want to see mine often. I love dressing my dolls up with different items from around my house, such as balloons and fabric scraps, so I might want to be a fashion designer. I also love drawing and learning how to make facial features and clothing look realistic in drawings, especially in anime, so I might want to do that. I have paper everywhere at my house with my drawings!

My family celebrates so many holidays. My dad is Jewish so we celebrate a few of the Jewish holidays, such as Hanukkah and Passover. My mom is Christian so we also celebrate Christian holidays. **I really enjoy being so diverse because I get to be different from other people.**

I am sweet like a bee.

SHAKTHISRI'S LITTLE WORLD

Shakthisri Saravanan

My mom used to say that a raindrop turned into a pearl on December 26th, 2013. Yes, I was born in India in a place called Coimbatore, Tamil Nadu (southern part of India) and my parents named me "Shakthisri." My dad told me that my name means "Energy, Strength, Power," which is also a Hindu goddess's name. My mom went to India to be with my grandparents and relatives so that they all could see me when I was born. However, I came to the USA when I was three months old.

We are a lovely family of four; Mom, Dad, me, and my little brother. His name is Siddharth and we all call him "Siddhu." Our family is a traditional Tamil family. Tamil is one of the world's classical languages and the oldest spoken language. I have been learning to read and write Tamil for the past four years. I love to read a lot of books. The novel "Pashmina" is my favorite book. I love drawing and arts. I wish to become an artist and a story writer when I grow up. I love winter, because I am a winter baby and love the holiday season with snow.

Our Tamil culture is very rich in traditions and celebrations. We have so many festivals and Pongal is my favorite one. It is a four-day festival that is like Thanksgiving for Sun God, Ox, and Cow. My family together cooks Pongal, which is a sweet dish made of milk, sugar, and rice. We eat sugarcane and delicious traditional food made by Mommy. I love spending time with friends and families and visiting the temple. Like Pongal, all our festivals have delicious foods and new dresses. These bring love and happiness.

I love to explore more about all cultures and make new friends every day!!

Happy Pongal!

On the day of the Pongal festival!!

Shreenika Patil

HAPPINESS IS BEING MYSELF!

In the year 2012, on the 17th day of February, a Maharashtrian couple in Mumbai, India, was blessed with an adorable and charming baby girl. That's me! **My name is Shreenika Sandeep Patil. I am named after a Hindu goddess, Mahalaxmi,** who is the goddess of abundance and prosperity.

I am a ten-year-old, empathetic, compassionate, loving being, often described as a free child (spontaneous, intuitive, creative) by my parents.

I am a nature-loving person. I love butterflies, birds, and pet animals (especially cats).

I love to be myself and speak my mind, and I always like to stand up for people.

My hobbies are piano, caricature, sketching, journaling and writing poems. I have been playing piano since I was six and can pick up any tune in five minutes just after listening to it.

I love to connect with my inner-self through meditation (chakra meditation) and breathwork.

I am an ardent reader and my Grandma says, I don't read books, I eat them. My favorite genres are realistic fiction, spirituality, fantasy, and graphic novels and my favorite authors are J.K. Rowling, Sri M, Kate DiCamillo, and Dave Pilkey.

Pani puri is my favorite Indian food. My mom makes the best pani puri and I, along with my dad, help her by eating it. I love pani puri so much that I can eat it daily.

I have received a bunch of prizes for my performances in stage plays and various competitions.

Every year I set a new goal on my birthday and try to accomplish it. Last year, I learned how to swim, and this year, my goal is to become a skillful basketball player.

I feel we all are beautiful, unique individuals in our own way and should love and accept each other the way we are.

Me and my friend, Blue Morpho!

Shrestha Chinthapalli

Crazy Shrestha.

AMMU STORY

My name is Shrestha. My favorite foods are brownies and Nutella. My family calls me Ammu, but my real name is Shrestha.

I am Indian. The place I was born is India. The first time I came to America was when I was one and a half years old. I have a mom, a dad, and an older brother in seventh grade. I speak an Indian language called Telugu.

My favorite colors are pink, purple, and blue, and I am very imaginative. I have millions of friends and I am very happy about that. I love to play with my friends and say yes whenever I get the chance.

My brother is funny and annoying occasionally. He is my friend and then he is my enemy. **My family is awesome and I am really happy about it.**

I AM SHRIANSH

S	Smart
H	Humorous
R	Respectful
I	Intelligent
A	Amazing
N	Nice
S	Super
H	Hardworking

Shriansh Tandon

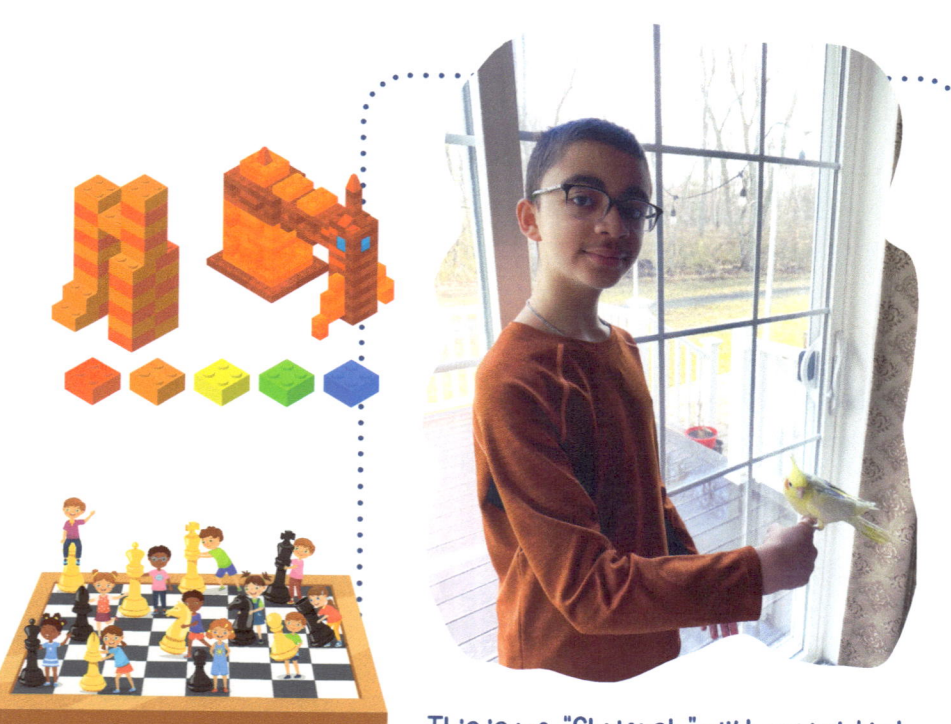

This is me, "Shriansh," with my pet bird, "Neo," who is an awesome cockatiel.

My name is Shriansh, I am in fifth grade, and I am ten years old. I was born in October on a snowy day in Canada. I have a younger brother named Ashwin. We both play together, as well as fight with each other, but more than that we love each other a lot. My favorite color is orange, even though I am allergic to oranges. I like to eat bananas. My classmates call me "Shri," but my friends in my neighborhood call me "Shreyray." My favorite indoor activities are chess, building Lego kits, table-tennis, Uno, and Bay-blades. My favorite outdoor activities are soccer and tennis. I play piano and my favorite song is called "Fur Elise." On special occasions I like to groove to music. My favorite moves are Orange Justice, Floss and Dab. My favorite ice cream is mint flavored. I have a pet cockatiel named Neo from

Neowise the comet. My religion is Hindu and my favorite festival is Diwali. And I celebrate festivals of other religions too. **When I grow up, I want to become a Lego designer because you get to play with Lego sets for a living.**

I AM SIMONE

Simone Kaur

Hi, my name is Simone Kaur. I was born on January 18, 2011, in Connecticut, and I'm in fifth grade. Not many people know this, but before I turned one, I had lived in three different countries: the United States, India, and Canada. The credit goes to my dad's job. But when I was almost two years old, we moved back to Connecticut and have lived there ever since.

I love to play basketball, whether it's during a game, or when I'm playing outside with my friends. I'm also really good at art. I love being creative and making drawings or paintings. Another thing that I am passionate about is music. I've loved singing ever since I was little. I also play the ukulele and hope to learn to play the guitar one day.

My parents, Sumandeep Kaur and Harvinder Singh, are from India, and they speak Hindi and Punjabi. I think it's really cool that my parents can speak three languages since they also speak English. I also have an older brother, Kabir, who is fifteen years old. A few words to describe my brother are funny, smart, and a football-lover. The rest of my family still lives in India. We still make sure to FaceTime them often, and sometimes they come here, or we visit them.

My family and I love to play board games. We play a lot of board games and card games. My family and I also love to go to different places. I like to travel, and I believe that traveling creates the most valuable memories. We've been to Florida, Hershey Park in Pennsylvania, and more. **I love to spend time with my family.**

The top left picture is of my family and me celebrating Diwali. On Diwali, we light fireworks and have a lot of Indian sweets. Celebrating Diwali is super fun.

THIS IS ME, PRINCESS SIYA

Siya Patel

This is me dressed in my traditional outfit for my uncle's wedding, just like a princess.

My name is Siya Patel. Siya means Sita (an Indian goddess and wife of Lord Ram). I am six years old. I live with Mommy, Daddy, and my grandparents. Other than English, I can also speak Gujarati, which is not just our first language but also something which keeps me connected with my grandparents, as they don't understand English that well.

Do you know my daddy and I share the same birthday, January 8th? Isn't that cool?! I have a big family, so most of the weekends we spend together by having parties, celebrations, and going out on vacations. I consider myself blessed to be surrounded by both grandparents, aunts, uncles, and cousins. I, being the youngest, get all the pampering and love.

We celebrate all holidays together, but my favorite of all is Diwali, which is the festival of lights. On this day I go to the temple with my family to pray, decorate our house with lights, do fireworks, get gifts, and eat a lot of sweets made by my granny. I love helping Mommy in the kitchen and playing with dolls in my little Barbie house.

I love all my friends and family!!

This photo was taken in April 2022, at sunset, on Nokomis Beach in Florida. This is me, my mom, and my dad.

I AM SKYE

My name is Skye. I am eight years old. I was born in Hartford, Connecticut, on March 15, 2014. I got my name from the Isle of Skye in Scotland because I'm part Scottish. My parents also really like islands so I think that helped too. My family is made up of me, my mom, my dad, and hopefully someday, a dog. My family and I love to travel and listen to music together. I have been taking drum lessons for several years. My favorite song to play on the drums is Come Together by The Beatles. Some of my favorite places that I have traveled to with my family are Arizona, the Caribbean, Florida, Mexico, California, and lots of places in between. When I'm traveling, some of my favorite things to do are collecting things down by the beach and going fishing. One of my most favorite fishing memories is catching a dogfish shark down by the beach. One time, when visiting my grandparents in Florida I even found shark teeth in the sand. My family is unique because we like to explore the world together. **We love seeing new places and making memories.**

Tanay Srivastava

ME AND MY WORLD!

My name is Tanay. The meaning of my name is "Son of the Family." I was born on August 16, 2012, in Hyderabad, India. I am in fourth grade. I live with my parents and my sister in South Windsor, Connecticut. My grandparents and extended family live in India. Being the youngest, I am the most loved one in the family, but sometimes I wonder if my sister is the favorite one or if I am. Well, this debate will go on forever.

I love spending time with my family. We love playing together; cricket, badminton, foosball, board games, cards, bike riding, and more! In most of the games, my sister and I team up and win. During my "me time," I love playing with Lego sets, video games, drawing and reading books. I am learning karate, chess, and swimming. My goal is to become a black belt in karate. My favorite subjects are math and science. I am learning to play trumpet and piano. I am a big fan of "dinosaurs." I want to study more about dinosaurs and want to become a "Paleontologist." I also like robotics and want to become an Engineer. So, I am confused, but I will figure it out once I grow up!

We celebrate the Indian festivals Diwali and Holi. Holi is my favorite festival. We cook many different types of Indian sweets and dishes. The best part of Holi is playing with colors and water. My favorite food is paneer and naan. I also like pizza.

I love traveling. I have visited Sydney, New York, Miami, Orlando, Key West, Tampa, Washington DC, Los Angeles, Las Vegas, Grand Canyon, and many more. I like traveling by airplanes more than cars. In airplanes we get to watch movies and get a lot of snacks. I am a good friend because I listen and care for others. I am respectful and try to make new friends. I love my family, friends, and school. I am Tanay!

I am Tanay, I love doing a lot of things. Here are a few pictures of me having fun!

I am Tanay and I love doing a lot of things. Here are a few pictures of me having fun!

I wish I could have this cake for my birthday.

Happy Birthday

Tingya Tang

I AM TINGYA

"你好 (ni hao)! **My name is Tingya Tang (汤听雅), but my dad likes to call me Ting-gu-ta simply because it sounds silly.** I have a twin brother Bowen; I was born two minutes earlier than him. I think my parents are the greatest because they have us. My parents came from China, but we were born in Manchester, CT. I like to adventure around, and I can't wait for the COVID virus to go away so we can go to far places like to Disney World because I can't wait to meet Elsa. I would really like to go to China to see my grandparents whom I haven't met yet. Yellowstone is off my list right now because I'm afraid of the volcanos.

I love my silly daddy; I feel very safe when he is around. I love my fun mommy; she always acts like a nurse when we get boo boos. I love my cool brother; he always tries to protect me when I'm scared of bugs. I love my grandma; she can make the best dumplings in the world. I love myself; I'm pretty, like to tell jokes, and love flowers.

I never want to leave this beautiful and lovely family.

Triguna Areti

THROUGH LIFE

Hi! My name is Triguna Areti! I am an American-Indian girl that is seven years old and will be turning eight on September 27th! I am amazing at writing, reading, and playing.

I have a sister that is four years older than me. Her name is Bhuvana Areti. I have great parents that take care of me really well. You can describe my family as loving, caring, and helpful, in my point of view!

I have gone to two different schools. The first one I went to was Breakthrough North School. I went there for Pre-K3, Pre-K4 and kindergarten. So far, I have been in Pleasant Valley School for first grade, second grade, and I will go there till fifth grade, and then I will go to TEMS, maybe.

I am also creative. I also like PINK. I like almost everything! I am talented and eager to learn more. I love school because that is where I get part of my knowledge. I get other knowledge from my religion or my parents or maybe from the internet and many other places. I am a busy child. I have three additional classes outside of school and I will get more!

VISHNU

I am a little stubborn and also I am a teeny, tiny, bit messy. I also have medium-long hair that keeps on growing! I have awesome family, friends, and others. I am sometimes addicted to TV. I am, most of the time, a slow eater.

Also, I am devoted to the three main Hindu Gods. Their names are Lord Vishnu, Lord Brahma, and Lord Shiva. I learn prayers and chant to the GODS! They are the fountain-head of this whole huge universe!

BRAHMA

I also like music, such as American Music and Indian Classical Music, and I am learning Indian Classical Dance and Music. It is always fun!

I want to be an advanced teacher or an advanced writer when I grow older!

I love my life as much as possible from the bottom of my heart!

I am at the Hartford public library and enjoying nature.

SHIVA

I AM VAIBHAV

Vaibhav Singh

Back in 2011, the night was black. The moon gave a warm breeze. In a distant town of India, named Bokaro, stars gave their light. The night moon was a full moon. A boy came into this world, and nature shook at the feet of the child. Animals roared at his presence (somewhere). He was born at 7:30 p.m. He was none other than me, Vaibhav Singh. At home, I was called Rasgulla and Chiku. I was named Vaibhav, as I brought a wealth of happiness with me being the first child of my parents. My mom says that I was scheduled to come out in the world on Dec 21, but I, being so impatient, couldn't resist myself and rushed to come out on Dec 18. I still can't keep my patience and get too excited for all the fun activities. I love watching movies, doing science research, reading and exploring books, and playing soccer, badminton, and chess.

My family shifted to the U.S. when I was just six months old. I made lots of great friends in my neighborhood of Manchester. I still miss Arjun, especially as we shifted to South Windsor. I got a great companion, my true partner in crime, my loving brother in May 2015. We call him Sarthak in school and Meethu at home. He is everything I was looking forward to. We play, we fight, we trick each other, we eat, and we sleep together. It is so fun to be with him. He irritates me when I just want to sit. Also he consoles me when I get sad. He is a very caring brother and wants to share everything with me even if I am not interested.

When we go to India, we love playing with our cousin-brothers and sisters. I love Indian mangoes. My favorite holidays are Holi and Diwali. During Holi we celebrate with a lot of colors and music. This year we celebrated Holi at Vallabhdham Temple. We put colors on probably ninety percent of the people who we knew and didn't know. There were more than 2,000 people. At Diwali we celebrate the festival of light and we light fireworks all over. This festival happened because of Rama killing Ravvan, the bad demon. And the villagers lit the lights as a celebration. My fav hobbies are chess, badminton, rock collecting, science research, and many more.

I go to Pleasant Valley School in grade five. Next year, I will be going to Timothy Edward. I will miss Mrs McAndrew. **I am excited for fun and studying hard to solve math problems with great teaching staff.**

I am ten years old. I love playing chess and having fun with my brother Sarthak.

Vaishnavi Dingari

Me harvesting in my backyard garden.

That's me, Vaishnavi!! A happy and inspirational kid. **I am planning to make a difference in this world. I am me!!!**

I AM ME

Who am I? I am Vaishnavi Dingari! I was born on July 15, 2013, and I love our planet! I love to plant! Last summer, our family grew some vegetables in our backyard garden. Did you know that planting helps the earth? Plants also help animals, and some of my favorite animals are koalas and giraffes because they are herbivores.

Now, you want to know about my family, correct? I have a mom, dad, and a little brother named Vihas in my family. My little brother is five years old. My brother and I both play piano and cricket, and I am better than him at both cricket and playing piano—way, way, way better.

Ah, now you ask about my hobbies. Well, my hobbies are reading books and exploring science. While I read, I like to swing on our indoor swing or lay down on my back. Sometimes, I stare at the sky and ask questions about what I see. I like to do small chemistry experiments. Science is so much fun!

My other hobby is hiking with my Dad. I like hiking because we get to spend time in nature.

Though very spread out around the world, my family has one deep origin: India. We visit India usually during the summer break because then we won't have to be marked absent at school. From India, we get a series of comics called ACK (Amar Chitra Katha); it teaches Indian mythology and history in the form of comics!!

My little sister; a cute Bichon frise dog.

Vedanth Manchala

I AM VEDANTH

Hi! My name is Vedanth Manchala, and I was born on October 3, 2011. My parents said I had a historical birth. I didn't really get it for a long time though. I was supposed to be born in November, but somehow I was born one month earlier on October 3rd. When I was born, I was weak and sick. I had to go to a place called the NICU (Neonatal Intensive Care Unit).

Let's talk about some stuff that is less sad. My parents have also said that I am curious. I agree with them, really. If I had, I would say three words that describe me would be stubborn, bold, and lastly, same thing my parents said, curious. I have several goals in my life, so do my parents; they have many goals for me too. One of my goals is to become a lawyer and go to a good college such as Yale or Harvard. These colleges aren't the most realistic ones for people to go to, but it's my goal.

My family is one of the most important in my life and is also another topic to talk about. If you ask my dad, my mom, or my brother, "Do you think Vedanth loves and cares for you?" Well, it matters what I did that day, but really I do love them all. Oh, right, I forgot the most important person in my family, Lily. No, Lily is not my human baby sister. She's my cute puppy sister.

Well, this is all about me. I am Vedanth.

Vihaan Vinayak

I AM HAPPY THAT I AM ME.

Long, long ago, so long ago, well, not so long ago I guess 😊 , I came into this world on a very special day, November 16, 2012. You might think, why is that a special day? It is special because of me! I do not have any siblings, which, in a way, is great because I get all the love, 😉 but some days I feel it would have been nice to have a sibling. I love Harry Potter and I love to play (all day long, if I may add). I am a dreamer and that is why I strongly believe imagination can lead to anything. I am an avid reader and I swim and can play the guitar and the flute. I also love to dance, which I think I got from my mom. As you can see, I am a very busy person. I am very inquisitive and I talk a lot, which I enjoy by the way. When I was younger, (than what I am now), I came up with my own jokes, and even thought I should try my hand at being a stand-up comedian.

I want to be a physicist when I grow up. Someday in the future I would like to travel to Mars and find

This picture is from when I performed a Bollywood dance at an event for Diwali.

some form of life there. I love mythology and my favorite is Egyptian Mythology. I am smart and love to learn new things. I am adventurous and love to explore, which sometimes ends in what I would like to call 'Happy accidents.' I am kind and like to make everyone around me happy. I am a responsible kid, but careless too—one of the perks of being a kid!

Well, now that you know a lot about me, there is one more thing that you need to know.

I AM ORIGINAL AND I AM ME!

I AM ME

Vihas Dingari

I am Vihas. Vihas means happy. I am five years old, born on April 25, 2016. My favorite color is blue because it is a cool color.

I like to play with toys, stuffed animals, and Lego bricks, but sometimes I do reading and writing. I also like to watch cartoons. I ride my bike outside with my friends in the neighborhood in spring and summer.

I reuse things such as broken crayons, pencils, and markers.

I am learning Taekwondo, piano, and cricket along with my elder sister.

I play cricket better than my sister. I am left-handed, so my coach says I can play ball games well. I don't know that, but I only see that I play cricket better than my sister. But she says that she plays better.

Sometimes we fight, but most of the time we play together. I like my sister and my sister likes me!

I love to eat mac and cheese and pasta, and I like to drink mango juice.

I do not like to sleep because we can't play at that time if we sleep.

Playing with stuffed animals and rolling around in the bed are my favorites.

I read books, mostly about animals.

Vihas – Happy Kid

Vishakan Adhyarth Vinodkumar

My picture has glasses. It has trees around it. There is a sun in the corner. I am wearing a greenish-blue shirt. On the side of me, there are two trees. I am waving my hand. I have a sharp nose. My mouth is smiling. I have an oval-shaped face. On the sides there is grass.

ABOUT ME

Hello! My name is Vishak. My favorite dinosaur is the Indoraptor. My mom loves to play with me. Also, my dad loves to play with me. Another thing about my dad is he loves to trick me. Also, my mom loves to trick me. My favorite pet is a dog. I love dogs because they look so cute when they are puppies. Next my favorite color is blue. **I like to play with my friends and I like to play new games.**

IT'S ME, VRINDA VANAPARTHY

Vrinda Vanaparthy

Once upon a time, in the year 2013, on November 7, there was a cute, little girl (that's me Vrinda Vanaparthy, name of a Goddess) born to lovely parents, Ram and Sowmya. I have a cute, little sister, Vibha Vanaparthy. I am a third grader.

I am an Indian-American, and I like to celebrate all Indian festivals like Diwali and Pongal. Diwali (the festival of lights) is my favorite festival that we celebrate every year during November for three days. I love the firecrackers, having sweets, and yummy food that my mom makes. Laddu is my favorite sweet that is made with chickpea batter and sugar. I love to dress up in my Indian clothes that have gems and golden sequin with bright colors. We give gifts to friends and families.

My hobbies are dancing, biking around my community, playing tennis, chess, and coloring. Every Friday night my family plays board games and card games. Carrom Board is my favorite game that has coins (black, white and red) to put in a hole (that has a net to hold all the coins) using a striker. This game is very popular in the Indian Subcontinent. Whoever puts all their color coins and a red coin in is the winner.

Music is my favorite activity. I am learning Carnatic Music just like my cousins do. I would like to do a music concert with my cousins when I visit India.

I love to go to school. I love to learn a lot of things in school from my teacher. I learn to be respectful to elders, well-behaved, and to be loved by everyone.

This summer I am planning to make my own YouTube channel to show my hobbies and my dancing skills; this is still under construction. **When it is ready you can click on the bell icon to subscribe. The End!**

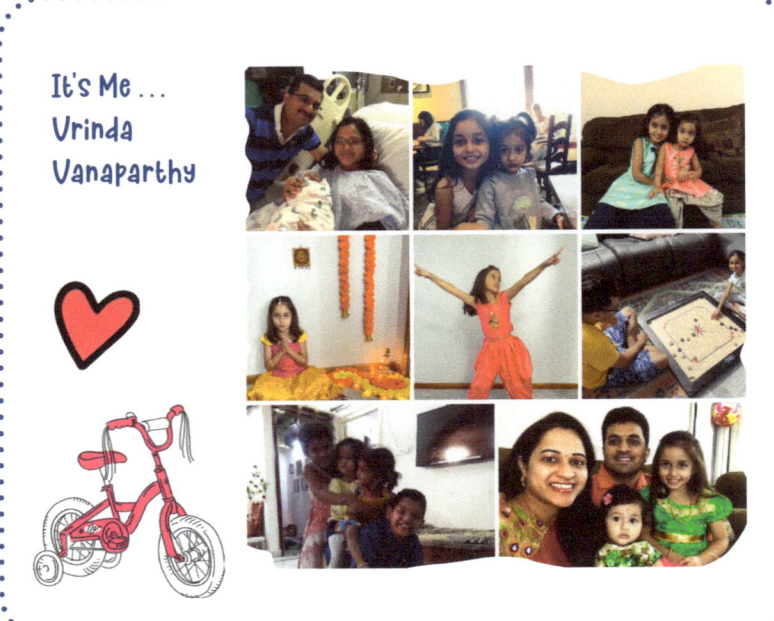

It's Me ...
Vrinda
Vanaparthy

Yelian Sofia Medina Cespedes

THE LIFE OF YELIAN

My full name is Yelián Sofía Medina Céspedes, and my middle name means Love Of Wisdom. I live with my mom, my dad, little sister Carla, and Dexter, our dog. I also have a brother that is older than me, and he works at a store. My brother lives in Arizona with his mother.

At home we speak Spanish because my dad made that rule for me to learn Spanish. I know a little bit of Spanish. My cousins and I speak English mostly, but the rest of the family speaks Spanish. I want to speak Spanish because I want to go to Puerto Rico and talk to my family. Many of them live there: my auntie Anneris, my two grandmas and grandpas, uncles, cousins, and many friends.

Something important about me is that I'm Christian and I am loved. Because of that, I got baptized on Sunday, April 17, 2022. And I love Jesus more than anything in the world. **I also like games like Roblox and YouTube and 5-minute crafts videos.**

This is me talking to my grandma in Spanish. I used to call her in the morning before going to school.

Yugesh Shanmuga Raja

I AM ME YUGESH

My name is Yugesh. My family calls me Yugi but my full name is Yugesh Shanmuga Raja. I am eight years old. I was born on February 23, 2014. This year I'm in second grade. I am in Mrs. Clauson's class, and Mrs. Clauson is a nice teacher.

My favorite food is pizza because it has a lot of cheese. I go to PV school, and my school is a very good school. I have a great family. My sister's name is Yuthika. She is in Timothy Edwards Middle School. My mom's name is Vinothini. My dad's name is Shanmuga Raja.

My favorite holiday is Diwali. Diwali is a great Indian festival. It means good over evil or fighting the darkness. My favorite number is 23 because I was born on February 23rd.

A thing that I like when spending time with my family is going out to fun places. For example, we went to New York and New Jersey and saw the Statue of Liberty up close! **We had to go to Liberty Island by ship. We enjoyed the trip.**

With My family!!

Zarah Killi

I AM ZARAH

Hi! My name is Zarah. I was born on July 2014. My name means brightness and princess, and by the way my hair is long like a princess 👸.

My family is made of my dad, my mom, my sister, myself, and my kitten Libby. I was born in America 🇺🇸 and my parents are from India 🇮🇳. My sister taught me how to fight (lol) and swim in the deep 🏊. My kitten sleeps next to me on my bed 🐈. I have a lot of family in India. My most favorite person in India is my cousin who is as old as me. As a family, we love to play games, watch Marvel movies, go on hikes and travel. My most favorite vacation was a Mexico cruise to the Bahamas. My mom and dad also speak Hindi, and my sister and I are learning.

My mom says I am stubborn, but I have a big heart. Do you want me to tell you what I love so so so so so so so so so so much? I love ART 💗. I know how to swim all strokes and I have been a part of a swim team for a year and our team won the championship. I love to read Dragon Master books 📚🐉. I am very choosy about my clothes and very picky about my food. I am learning gymnastics and Taekwondo. **I love play dates, pretend play, and sleepovers, but I am very loud.**

I love rides in Six flags.

ME AND MY FAMILY: THE THAKKAR'S

My name is Ziya and I am eight years old. Ziya means light. The right way to pronounce my name is with the short "I." I speak multiple languages and want to learn more. I want to be a doctor when I grow up because I like helping people. I want to help make people feel better. I like things to be perfect and sometimes take my own time to make it perfect.

I love art and drawing. I love colors and one of my favorite festivals is Holi, which is a festival of colors. My favorite color is aqua teal.

I live with my mom, my dad, and my younger sister, Shanaya. My sister and I were born in Hartford, Connecticut and our parents are from India. I love playing with my sister and we do most of the activities together.

My family believes in togetherness. We celebrate all our festivals together with family and friends. We worship together and enjoy everything that our culture brings to us. We have idols of gods at our home. My mom and I make the idols dress up with beautiful and decorative dresses. I love getting dressed up myself in our traditional wear. I love decorating my home during our festivities.

Ziya Thakkar

My family is vegetarian. My mom makes a variety of Indian food at home, and I love it. My favorite food is "Daal Dhokli," which is wheat flour pieces boiled in lentil soup. I sometimes help my mom to prepare food.

I love my school, Pleasant Valley Elementary School. **I love my school so much that I'm waiting for my sister to join it.**

This is me after my artwork. I was practicing doing shades in my art class.

Zoe Gnassounou

I AM ZOE GRACE

My Name is Zoe Grace, and I was born in Manchester Memorial Hospital in Connecticut on a sunny, June 6ᵗʰ day.
I live with my parents and my little brother named Ezra who is three years old. My parents are originally from Togo in West Africa and came to America a long time ago. They speak and write three languages; their native language is called Ewe, then French, and English, but I can understand and speak a little of Ewe. I also understand French, but I cannot speak it. Maybe when I grow up I will visit my cousins in France. I have many family members around the world. I would love to see all of them one day. Most of my family members (uncles and cousins) call me Zozo, short for Zoe and Adzo (Adzo is my native name for a girl born on Monday).

I love to play at the playground because I can make more friends and I love my friends in school too. I am in kindergarten, and it is the best thing ever because I like my teacher (Mrs. Victoria Parent is the best). I practice karate, too, to be stronger, and I just started practicing swimming, but I am a little bit scared of deep water.

One of my favorite toys is LOL Collections and I love everything about it. I can be picky sometimes when it

I love to ride bicycles with my brother, Ezra, and play at the playground because I can make more friends when I go there. My parents are originally from Togo in West Africa and came to America a long time ago. They speak and write three languages. Their native language is called Ewe, then French and English, but I can understand and speak a little of Ewe. Both my Grandparents live in Togo.

comes to food, but pasta is my favorite food. I love to make "Botokoin" and "Atchomon" (my favorite snacks from my parent's home country) with my brother. My mom calls me "Delali," my nickname, which means "Jesus is alive" in Ewe. My family is Christian, and we pray every day, and I love Jesus to be part of our lives to protect us from bad things. Both my grandparents live in Togo. My little brother and I call our grandmothers 'Meme' and grandfathers 'Pepe.' My grandmother used to visit with us, but because of COVID I have not seen them. I miss them a lot. I also love to read, and ride my bicycle. My dad and I play hide and seek with my little brother all the time and I love to hide in the closet.

I can make yummy waffles. Everybody loves my waffles.

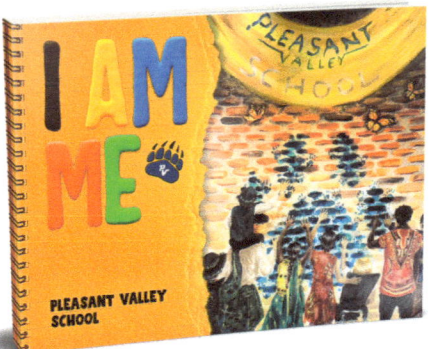

We hope you have enjoyed reading this collection, and learning more about the incredible students and families of Pleasant Valley School.

If you are interested in having Publish Your Purpose produce a similar book project for you and your school district, please contact **hello@publishyourpurpose.com**.

www.ingramcontent.com/pod-product-compliance
Lightning Source LLC
Chambersburg PA
CBHW040438150626

46551CB00024B/566